To

_____

From

_____

Message

_____

_____

_____

_____

Promises from God for Daily Living

© 2007 Christian Art Gifts, RSA
        Christian Art Gifts Inc., IL, USA

Compiled by Wilma Le Roux and Lynette Douglas
Designed by Christian Art Gifts

ISBN 978-1-86920-845-5

Printed in China

07 08 09 10 11 12 13 14 15 16 – 10 9 8 7 6 5 4 3 2 1

PROMISES
FROM GOD FOR
Daily Living

CONTENTS

Introduction

God is not a man, that he should lie, nor a son of man,
that he should change his mind. Does he speak and
then not act? Does he promise and not fulfill?
Numbers 23:19, NIV

The Bible is full of the promises of God – promises of majestic grandeur for times of global or national catastrophe, but also gentle promises for the everyday matters of daily life. And God's promises are not empty. They are based on His infinite love and faithfulness. God will do what He says. Our God is a faithful God, intimately concerned with the tiny details of our days. The goodness of God is found on every page of Scripture, and God is ready to answer our every need.

Whatever we do, whatever we face from day to day, we can find comfort and encouragement from God's Word to guide and sustain us, assured that as we turn to Him, saturating our lives with His promises, we will begin to live life abundantly, trusting in His goodness for all our needs.

$\mathcal{A}$NGER

He who is slow to anger is better than the mighty, and
he who rules his spirit than he who takes a city.
Proverbs 16:32, NKJV

People who anger easily, explode easily in fury. That is not the path of true love. Love never despairs about people and does not get impatient with them. When we lose our temper, we lose everything. If all around you people lose their heads and burst out in anger, love will enable you to remain calm, to judge things properly and to make the right decision. This is where Christian love is of immeasurable value in human relations.

The even-tempered person is not inclined to hatred and bitterness. He who is master of his temper can reach heights, enabling him to be master of anything. Through the Holy Spirit, we can use anger in our favor. It is an important part of spiritual growth to have your temper working for you instead of against you, and here love is of immeasurable value. It calms your emotions and helps you not to be easily angered.

The Word's answer

to anger

Be not hasty in thy spirit to be angry: for anger resteth in the bosom of fools.

Ecclesiastes 7:9, KJV

I will praise you, O LORD. Although you were angry with me, your anger has turned away and you have comforted me.

Isaiah 12:1, NIV

But You are God, ready to pardon, gracious and merciful, slow to anger, abundant in kindness, and did not forsake them.

Nehemiah 9:17, NKJV

For his anger is but for a moment, and his favor is for a lifetime. Weeping may tarry for the night, but joy comes with the morning.

Psalm 30:5, ESV

The LORD is compassionate and gracious, slow to anger, abounding in love. He will not always accuse, nor will he harbor his anger forever.

Psalm 103:8-9, NIV

Good sense makes one slow to anger, and it is his glory to overlook an offense.

Proverbs 19:11, ESV

"But I tell you that anyone who is angry with his brother will be subject to judgment."

Matthew 5:22, NIV

But now ye also put off all these; anger, wrath, malice, blasphemy, filthy communication out of your mouth.

Colossians 3:8, KJV

Let all bitterness and wrath and anger and clamor and slander be put away from you, along with all malice.

Ephesians 4:31, ESV

"But I say unto you, Love your enemies, bless them that curse you, do good to them that hate you, and pray for them which despitefully use you, and persecute you; that ye may be the children of your Father which is in heaven: for he maketh his sun to rise on the evil and on the good, and sendeth rain on the just and on the unjust."

Matthew 5:44-45, KJV

"In your anger do not sin": Do not let the sun go down while you are still angry, and do not give the devil a foothold.

Ephesians 4:26-27, NIV

Beloved, never avenge yourselves, but leave it to the wrath of God, for it is written, "Vengeance is mine, I will repay, says the Lord." To the contrary, "if your enemy is hungry, feed him; if he is thirsty, give him something to drink; for by so doing you will heap burning coals on his head."

Romans 12:19-20, ESV

So then, my beloved brethren, let every man be swift to hear, slow to speak, slow to wrath; for the wrath of man does not produce the righteousness of God.

James 1:19-20, NKJV

A soft answer turneth away wrath: but grievous words stir up anger.

Proverbs 15:1, KJV

Refrain from anger, and forsake wrath! Fret not yourself; it tends only to evil.

Psalm 37:8, ESV

CONTENTMENT

In peace I will both lie down and sleep; for you alone,
O LORD, make me dwell in safety.
Psalm 4:8, ESV

How can you live sweetly amid the vexatious
things, the irritating things, the multitude
of little worries and frets that lie all along
your way, and that you cannot evade? You
cannot at present change your surroundings.
Whatever kind of life you are to live, must
be lived amid precisely the experiences in
which you are now moving. Here you must
win your victories or suffer your defeats.
No restlessness or discontent can change
your lot. Others may have other circumstances surrounding them, but here are
yours. You had better make up your mind
to accept what you cannot alter. You can
live a beautiful life in the midst of your
present circumstances.

Contentment from the Word

Whoever listens to me will live in safety and be at ease, without fear of harm.

Proverbs 1:33, NIV

Keep your life free from love of money, and be content with what you have, for he has said, "I will never leave you nor forsake you."

Hebrews 13:5, ESV

But my God shall supply all your need according to his riches in glory by Christ Jesus.

Philippians 4:19, KJV

I have learned to be content whatever the circumstances. I know what it is to be in need, and I know what it is to have plenty. I have learned the secret of being content in any and every situation, whether well fed or hungry, whether living in plenty or in want.

Philippians 4:11-12, NIV

There is nothing better for a man, than that he should eat and drink, and that he should make his soul enjoy good in his labour. This also I saw, that it was from the hand of God.

Ecclesiastes 2:24, KJV

My soul shall be satisfied as with marrow and fatness, and my mouth shall praise You with joyful lips.

Psalm 63:5, NKJV

Now there is great gain in godliness with contentment, for we brought nothing into the world, and we cannot take anything out of the world.

1 Timothy 6:6-7, ESV

The fear of the LORD leads to life: Then one rests content, untouched by trouble.

Proverbs 19:23, NIV

And the soldiers likewise demanded of him, saying, "And what shall we do?" And he said unto them, "Do violence to no man, neither accuse *any* falsely; and be content with your wages."

Luke 3:14, KJV

He that loveth silver shall not be satisfied with silver; nor he that loveth abundance with increase: this is also vanity.

Ecclesiastes 5:10, KJV

But if we have food and clothing, with these we will be content.

1 Timothy 6:8, ESV

But Esau said, "I have enough, my brother; keep what you have for yourself."

Genesis 33:9, ESV

Rest in the LORD, and wait patiently for Him; Do not fret because of him who prospers in his way, Because of the man who brings wicked schemes to pass.

Psalm 37:7, NKJV

The fruit of righteousness will be peace; the effect of righteousness will be quietness and confidence forever.

Isaiah 32:17, NIV

I am still confident of this: I will see the goodness of the LORD in the land of the living. Wait for the LORD; be strong and take heart and wait for the LORD.

Psalm 27:13-14, NIV

COURAGE

I can do all things through Christ which strengtheneth me.

Philippians 4:13, KJV

Courage takes many forms. In hospital wards and sick rooms there are courageous fighters. Our towns and cities are full of people who quietly struggle for a dignified human existence day after day. They maintain integrity and self-respect in the face of apparently insurmountable problems. Courage comes to the fore when everything seems lost and all hope seems gone. The courageous person remains steadfast when all others begin to despair.

Where does this kind of courage come from? It is the determination to conquer that calls forth a very special kind of perseverence in the moment of testing. Real courage has its origins deep in a person's heart and is often fuelled by love and trust.

When your spirit is in harmony with the Holy Spirit your life is filled with a holy strength that enables you to face life with courage and confidence.

Courage from
the Word

Be strong and of a good courage, fear not, nor be afraid of them: for the LORD thy God, he it is that doth go with thee; he will not fail thee, nor forsake thee.

Deuteronomy 31:6, KJV

"Be strong and of good courage; do not be afraid, nor be dismayed, for the LORD your God is with you wherever you go."

Joshua 1:9, NKJV

Wait on the LORD: be of good courage, and he shall strengthen thine heart: wait, I say, on the LORD.

Psalm 27:14, KJV

But now thus says the LORD, he who created you, O Jacob, he who formed you, O Israel: "Fear not, for I have redeemed you; I have called you by name, you are mine."

Isaiah 43:1, ESV

Be of good courage, and He shall strengthen your heart, all you who hope in the LORD.

Psalm 31:24, NKJV

The Lord is on my side; I will not fear: what can man do unto me? The Lord taketh my part with them that help me: therefore shall I see my desire upon them that hate me. It is better to trust in the Lord than to put confidence in man.

Psalm 118:6-8, KJV

"I have told you these things, so that in me you may have peace. In this world you will have trouble. But take heart! I have overcome the world."

John 16:33, NIV

For God has not given us a spirit of fear, but of power and of love and of a sound mind.

2 Timothy 1:7, NKJV

Therefore do not throw away your confidence, which has a great reward. For you have need of endurance, so that when you have done the will of God you may receive what is promised.

Hebrews 10:35-36, ESV

Why art thou cast down, O my soul? and why art thou disquieted within me? hope thou in God: for I shall yet praise him, who is the health of my countenance, and my God.

Psalm 42:11, KJV

The wicked flee when no one pursues, but the righteous are bold as a lion.

Proverbs 28:1, NKJV

So we say with confidence, "The Lord is my helper; I will not be afraid. What can man do to me?"

Hebrews 13:6, NIV

Be strong and courageous. Do not be afraid or discouraged because of the king of Assyria and the vast army with him, for there is greater power with us than with him. With him is only the arm of flesh, but with us is the LORD our God to help us fight our battles.

2 Chronicles 32:7-8, NIV

$\mathcal{F}$AITH

Now faith is being sure of what we hope for and certain of what we do not see.

Hebrews 11:1, NIV

If your Christian faith is not applied practically, you have not yet understood the full message of Christ. He was preeminently a practical person. He talked about feeding the hungry, clothing the naked, visiting the prisoners and working to the glory of God. Love should find expression in service. The depth and quality of your love for and faith in Jesus Christ, will be revealed in the service that you render to others in His Name. It is through a combination of love and service that faith is cultivated and strengthened.

Love and service are the nutrients of a strong faith. If they are absent, your faith wanes and fails in the function which it should fulfil. If you desire to have a stronger faith, you must love God wholeheartedly and serve Him with greater enthusiasm. Sincere love for God and inspired service combine to create a positive faith. It leads you into a deeper fellowship with the Master.

Faith from
the Word

Jesus said unto him, "If thou canst believe, all things are possible to him that believeth."

Mark 9:23, KJV

But to all who did receive him, who believed in his name, he gave the right to become children of God.

John 1:12, ESV

"For God so loved the world, that he gave his only Son, that whoever believes in him should not perish but have eternal life."

John 3:16, ESV

For by grace you have been saved through faith, and that not of yourselves; it is the gift of God, not of works, lest anyone should boast.

Ephesians 2:8-9, NKJV

Jesus said to him, "Have you believed because you have seen me? Blessed are those who have not seen and yet have believed."

John 20:29, ESV

"And all things, whatsoever ye shall ask in prayer, believing, ye shall receive."

Matthew 21:22, KJV

"When a man believes in me, he does not believe in me only, but in the one who sent me. When he looks at me, he sees the one who sent me. I have come into the world as a light, so that no one who believes in me should stay in darkness."

John 12:44-46, NIV

So then faith cometh by hearing, and hearing by the word of God.

Romans 10:17, KJV

In all circumstances take up the shield of faith, with which you can extinguish all the flaming darts of the evil one.

Ephesians 6:16, ESV

You are all sons of God through faith in Christ Jesus.

Galatians 3:26, NIV

To him give all the prophets witness, that through his name whosoever believeth in him shall receive remission of sins.

Acts 10:43, KJV

I have been crucified with Christ; it is no longer I who live, but Christ lives in me; and the life which I now live in the flesh I live by faith in the Son of God, who loved me and gave Himself for me.

Galatians 2:20, NKJV

"For truly, I say to you, if you have faith like a mustard seed, you will say to this mountain, 'Move from here to there,' and it will move, and nothing will be impossible for you."

Matthew 17:20, ESV

"I tell you the truth, anyone who has faith in me will do what I have been doing. He will do even greater things than these, because I am going to the Father."

John 14:12, NIV

"Have faith in God. For assuredly, I say to you, whoever says to this mountain, 'Be removed and be cast into the sea,' and does not doubt in his heart, but believes that those things he says will be done, he will have whatever he says. Therefore I say to you, whatever things you ask when you pray, believe that you receive them, and you will have them."

Mark 11:22-24, NKJV

FAMILY

A father to the fatherless, a defender of widows, is God in his holy dwelling.

Psalm 68:5, NIV

What is a home? Is it a roof over your head to keep out the rain? Four walls to ward of the biting wind? A floor, a door, windows? A home is a baby's smile, a mother's song, a child's laughter, a father's protection. It is the warmth of loving hearts, the light in joyful eyes, friendliness, faithfulness, cameraderie, and love. A home is the first school and the first church that a child knows. It is here that she learns what is good, and precious, and right. Here each family member can find comfort when life hurts them.

A home is where joy and sadness are shared, where love and respect are found, here friends are always welcome. Here the most simple meal is a banquet fit for royalty because it was honestly earned and prepared with love. Most of all, home is a place where family worship links hearts inextricably to each other and to God. And that is where God gives His blessing.

THE WORD'S VIEW

ON FAMILY

He grants the barren woman a home, like
a joyful mother of children.

Psalm 113:9, NKJV

Children's children are the crown of old
men; and the glory of children are their
fathers.

Proverbs 17:6, KJV

My son, keep your father's commands and
do not forsake your mother's teaching. Bind
them upon your heart forever; fasten them
around your neck.

Proverbs 6:20-21, NIV

Children, obey your parents in the Lord,
for this is right. "Honor your father and
mother" – which is the first commandment
with a promise – "that it may go well with
you and that you may enjoy long life on the
earth. Fathers, do not exasperate your children; instead, bring them up in the training
and instruction of the Lord.

Ephesians 6:1-4, NIV

Hear, my children, the instruction of a father, and give attention to know understanding; for I give you good doctrine: Do not forsake my law. When I was my father's son, tender and the only one in the sight of my mother, He also taught me, and said to me: "Let your heart retain my words; keep my commands, and live."

Proverbs 4:1-4, NKJV

For he who sanctifies and those who are sanctified all have one origin. That is why he is not ashamed to call them brothers.

Hebrews 2:11, ESV

A father of the fatherless, and a judge of the widows, is God in his holy habitation.

Psalm 68:5, KJV

Furthermore, we have had human fathers who corrected us, and we paid them respect. Shall we not much more readily be in subjection to the Father of spirits and live? For they indeed for a few days chastened us as seemed best to them, but He for our profit, that we may be partakers of His holiness.

Hebrews 12:9-10, NKJV

On you was I cast from my birth, and from my mother's womb you have been my God.

Psalm 22:10, ESV

And a crowd was sitting around him, and they said to him, "Your mother and your brothers are outside, seeking you." And he answered them, "Who are my mother and my brothers?" And looking about at those who sat around him, he said, "Here are my mother and my brothers! Whoever does the will of God, he is my brother and sister and mother."

Mark 3:32-35, ESV

As for me and my house, we will serve the LORD.

Joshua 24:15, KJV

Behold, children are a heritage from the LORD, The fruit of the womb is a reward. Like arrows in the hand of a warrior, So are the children of one's youth. Happy is the man who has his quiver full of them.

Psalm 127:3-5, NKJV

FATIGUE

The LORD is my shepherd; I shall not want. He maketh me to lie down in green pastures: he leadeth me beside the still waters. He restoreth my soul.

Psalm 23:1-3, KJV

It seems that life is lived at a faster and faster pace each day. We rush from one event to another, and hardly have time to breathe, let alone focus on God. A common complaint is one of weariness. We are worn out by the demands of life. And too often we prop ourselves up with energy drinks and pep pills.

But God has promised to refresh us in our weariness. When we spend time in God's presence, He gives us His rest and peace and reorders our priorities. Then when we do what He has shown us is important, He also gives us the strength to see those tasks through. The best thing to do when you have too much to do is take a little time to talk to God, and He will renew and refresh you, exchanging your fatigue for His strength.

COMFORT FOR

THE FATIGUED

The everlasting God, the LORD, the Creator of the ends of the earth, neither faints nor is weary. His understanding is unsearchable. He gives power to the weak, and to those who have no might He increases strength. Even the youths shall faint and be weary, and the young men shall utterly fall, but those who wait on the LORD shall renew their strength; they shall mount up with wings like eagles, they shall run and not be weary, they shall walk and not faint.

Isaiah 40:28-31, NKJV

For which cause we faint not; but though our outward man perish, yet the inward man is renewed day by day.

2 Corinthians 4:16, KJV

"Come to Me, all you who labor and are heavy laden, and I will give you rest. Take My yoke upon you and learn from Me, for I am gentle and lowly in heart, and you will find rest for your souls. For My yoke is easy and My burden is light."

Matthew 11:28-30, NKJV

I myself will tend my sheep and have them lie down, declares the Sovereign LORD. I will search for the lost and bring back the strays. I will bind up the injured and strengthen the weak, but the sleek and the strong I will destroy. I will shepherd the flock with justice.

Ezekiel 34:15-16, NIV

Six days thou shalt do thy work, and on the seventh day thou shalt rest: that thine ox and thine ass may rest, and the son of thy handmaid, and the stranger, may be refreshed.

Exodus 23:12, KJV

"For I will satisfy the weary soul, and every languishing soul I will replenish."

Jeremiah 31:25, ESV

There remains therefore a rest for the people of God. For he who has entered His rest has himself also ceased from his works as God did from His. Let us therefore be diligent to enter that rest, lest anyone fall according to the same example of disobedience.

Hebrews 4:9-11, NKJV

God will speak to this people, to whom he said, "This is the resting place, let the weary rest"; and, "This is the place of repose."

Isaiah 28:11-12, NIV

Repent therefore, and turn again, that your sins may be blotted out, that times of refreshing may come from the presence of the Lord.

Acts 3:19-20, ESV

In vain you rise early and stay up late, toiling for food to eat – for he grants sleep to those he loves.

Psalm 127:2, NIV

When thou liest down, thou shalt not be afraid: yea, thou shalt lie down, and thy sleep shall be sweet.

Proverbs 3:24, KJV

The sleep of a laborer is sweet, whether he eats little or much.

Ecclesiastes 5:12, NIV

At this I awoke and looked around. My sleep had been pleasant to me.

Jeremiah 31:26, NIV

$\mathcal{F}$EAR

I sought the LORD, and he answered me and delivered me from all my fears.

Psalm 34:4, ESV

Fear stalks its prey in every area of life: through sickness or death, through insecurity, family or financial problems, unemployment. Each of these can generate its own fear, robbing you of peace of mind. Once you are caught in the web of fear, it can have devastating physical, intellectual, and spiritual consequences.

Unconditional and total trust in God's omnipotent power through Jesus Christ, is the only trustworthy protection against the evil of fear. Only through Him are you able to overcome every problem as it arises. Hold on to Christ in love and faith. Pray without ceasing. Develop a deep and consistent awareness of His presence. Then you will be assured peace of mind and security. Love is the best antidote for fear. As John says, *"There is no fear in love. But perfect love drives out fear"* (1 Jn. 4:18, NIV).

Overcoming

FEAR

Fear not, for I am with you; be not dismayed, for I am your God. I will strengthen you, yes, I will help you, I will uphold you with My righteous right hand.

Isaiah 41:10, NKJV

For I am persuaded, that neither death, nor life, nor angels, nor principalities, nor powers, nor things present, nor things to come, nor height, nor depth, nor any other creature, shall be able to separate us from the love of God, which is in Christ Jesus our Lord.

Romans 8:38-39, KJV

When I am afraid, I will trust in you. In God, whose word I praise, in God I trust; I will not be afraid. What can mortal man do to me?

Psalm 56:3-4, NIV

The LORD is my light and my salvation; whom shall I fear? the LORD is the strength of my life; of whom shall I be afraid?

Psalm 27:1, KJV

It is the LORD who goes before you. He will be with you; he will not leave you or forsake you. Do not fear or be dismayed.

Deuteronomy 31:8, ESV

Yea, though I walk through the valley of the shadow of death, I will fear no evil: for thou art with me; thy rod and thy staff they comfort me.

Psalm 23:4, KJV

You will not fear the terror of the night, nor the arrow that flies by day, nor the pestilence that stalks in darkness, nor the destruction that wastes at noonday. A thousand may fall at your side, ten thousand at your right hand, but it will not come near you. For he will command his angels concerning you to guard you in all your ways.

Psalm 91:5-7, 11, ESV

When you pass through the waters, I will be with you; and when you pass through the rivers, they will not sweep over you. When you walk through the fire, you will not be burned; the flames will not set you ablaze. Do not be afraid, for I am with you.

Isaiah 43:2, 5, NIV

And he said unto them, "Why are ye so fearful? how is it that ye have no faith?"

Mark 4:40, KJV

For you did not receive the spirit of bondage again to fear, but you received the Spirit of adoption by whom we cry out, "Abba, Father."

Romans 8:15, NKJV

For God hath not given us the spirit of fear; but of power, and of love, and of a sound mind.

2 Timothy 1:7, KJV

There is no fear in love; but perfect love casteth out fear: because fear hath torment. He that feareth is not made perfect in love.

1 John 4:18, KJV

The name of the LORD is a strong tower: the righteous runneth into it, and is safe.

Proverbs 18:10, KJV

But you are a shield around me, O LORD; you bestow glory on me and lift up my head.

Psalm 3:3, NIV

ℱORGIVENESS

"I, I am he who blots out your transgressions for my own sake, and I will not remember your sins."

Isaiah 43:25, ESV

We have become so used to the thought of God's pardon that the cost and wonder of it tend to be forgotten. That God whom we have so offended in thought, word and deed should forgive us at all is wonderful, especially when we remember that His moral nature demands that He not pass lightly over our rebellious acts and attitude. But by the substitution of His Son to bear the due punishment of our sins, God can now be just and yet the Justifier of the one who believes in Jesus.

God has not only forgiven us but does it with a generosity that is so attractive and exalting that we can only worship and adore Him. With everlasting kindness He pities and pardons us, and when He forgives it is with completeness and finality. Happy are we whose sin is removed. We are forgiven for Christ's sake.

GOD'S PROMISES

OF FORGIVENESS

"But I say unto you, Love your enemies, bless them that curse you, do good to them that hate you, and pray for them which despitefully use you, and persecute you; That ye may be the children of your Father which is in heaven: for he maketh his sun to rise on the evil and on the good, and sendeth rain on the just and on the unjust."

Matthew 5:44-45, KJV

"For if you forgive men their trespasses, your heavenly Father will also forgive you. But if you do not forgive men their trespasses, neither will your Father forgive your trespasses."

Matthew 6:14-15, NKJV

"Pay attention to yourselves! If your brother sins, rebuke him, and if he repents, forgive him, and if he sins against you seven times in the day, and turns to you seven times, saying, 'I repent,' you must forgive him."

Luke 17:3-4, ESV

"Do not judge, and you will not be judged. Do not condemn, and you will not be condemned. Forgive, and you will be forgiven."

Luke 6:37, NIV

And you, being dead in your trespasses and the uncircumcision of your flesh, He has made alive together with Him, having forgiven you all trespasses, having wiped out the handwriting of requirements that was against us, which was contrary to us. And He has taken it out of the way, having nailed it to the cross.

Colossians 2:13-14, NKJV

Peter came to Jesus and asked, "Lord, how many times shall I forgive my brother when he sins against me? Up to seven times?" Jesus answered, "I tell you, not seven times, but seventy-seven times."

Matthew 18:21-22, NIV

And when ye stand praying, forgive, if ye have aught against any; that your Father also which is in heaven may forgive you your trespasses. But if ye do not forgive, neither will your Father which is in heaven forgive your trespasses.

Mark 11:25-26, KJV

Blessed is he whose transgressions are forgiven, whose sins are covered. Blessed is the man whose sin the LORD does not count against him and in whose spirit is no deceit.

Psalm 32:1-2, NIV

For thou, LORD, art good, and ready to forgive; and plenteous in mercy unto all them that call upon thee.

Psalm 86:5, KJV

And be kind to one another, tenderhearted, forgiving one another, even as God in Christ forgave you.

Ephesians 4:32, NKJV

All we like sheep have gone astray; we have turned every one to his own way; and the LORD hath laid on him the iniquity of us all.

Isaiah 53:6, KJV

Have mercy on me, O God, according to your steadfast love; according to your abundant mercy blot out my transgressions. Wash me thoroughly from my iniquity, and cleanse me from my sin!

Psalm 51:1-2, ESV

FRIENDSHIP

"Greater love has no one than this, that someone lays down his life for his friends. You are my friends if you do what I command you."

John 15:13-14, ESV

A friend is someone whose company you wish to enjoy as long as you live. It is someone you turn to when you go through hard times and who will sincerely share in your joy and good fortune.

You can lean on your friend when your heart is breaking, and when you are on your feet again, he will forget about your weakness. He prays for you when life has dealt you a blow, and rejoices when things go well.

Your friend marvels at your good qualities and loves you in spite of your faults. He is proud when you achieve your goals, but is not ashamed of you when you fail. He will speak the truth, even though it might hurt, and you can tell him the truth without offending him. A friend does not need to prove his friendship, but he will.

THE WORD'S VIEW

ON FRIENDSHIP

A man of many companions may come to ruin, but there is a friend who sticks closer than a brother.

Proverbs 18:24, NIV

Two are better than one; because they have a good reward for their labour. For if they fall, the one will lift up his fellow: but woe to him that is alone when he falleth; for he hath not another to help him up. Again, if two lie together, then they have heat: but how can one be warm alone? And if one prevail against him, two shall withstand him; and a threefold cord is not quickly broken.

Ecclesiastes 4:9-12, KJV

My intercessor is my friend as my eyes pour out tears to God; on behalf of a man he pleads with God as a man pleads for his friend.

Job 16:20-21, NIV

"For where two or three come together in my name, there am I with them."

Matthew 18:20, NIV

Then Jonathan said to David, "Go in peace, because we have sworn both of us in the name of the LORD, saying, 'The LORD shall be between me and you, and between my offspring and your offspring, forever.'"

1 Samuel 20:42, ESV

Bear one another's burdens, and so fulfill the law of Christ.

Galatians 6:2, ESV

Ointment and perfume rejoice the heart: so doth the sweetness of a man's friend by hearty counsel.

Proverbs 27:9, KJV

I am a friend to all who fear you, to all who follow your precepts.

Psalm 119:63, NIV

"No longer do I call you servants, for the servant does not know what his master is doing; but I have called you friends, for all that I have heard from my Father I have made known to you."

John 15:15, ESV

He who loves purity of heart and has grace
on his lips, the king will be his friend.

Proverbs 22:11, NKJV

The friendship of the LORD is for those who
fear him, and he makes known to them his
covenant.

Psalm 25:14, ESV

And the scripture was fulfilled that says,
"Abraham believed God, and it was credited
to him as righteousness," and he was called
God's friend.

James 2:23, NIV

A friend loveth at all times, and a brother
is born for adversity.

Proverbs 17:17, KJV

Dear friends, let us love one another, for
love comes from God. Everyone who loves
has been born of God and knows God.

1 John 4:7, NIV

$\mathcal{G}$IVING

Good will come to him who is generous and lends
freely, who conducts his affairs with justice.

Psalm 112:5, NIV

When a gift is given freely and with joy, the value of the gift is increased. It is the privilege of every Christian to be a giver. When the Holy Spirit of the living Christ flows through you, He teaches you to love and withhold nothing that will bless and enrich your neighbor. Your purpose in life is to be a blessing to others. Let your gift always be accompanied by a prayer of thanksgiving and a desire that God will bless the gift, and thank Him that you are able to give.

The most important gift that you can offer is yourself. God has given you a personality and you must do your very best to develop it to His glory and to the service of others. That is something that every Christian can offer his fellowmen – regardless of their financial position or social standing.

God gives freely, without any obligations, and you and I should do the same.

The Word's view

on giving

Whoever despises his neighbor is a sinner, but blessed is he who is generous to the poor.

Proverbs 14:21, ESV

"Thus, when you give to the needy, sound no trumpet before you, as the hypocrites do in the synagogues and in the streets, that they may be praised by others. Truly, I say to you, they have received their reward. But when you give to the needy, do not let your left hand know what your right hand is doing, so that your giving may be in secret. And your Father who sees in secret will reward you."

Matthew 6:2-4, ESV

Command those who are rich in this present age not to be haughty, nor to trust in uncertain riches but in the living God, who gives us richly all things to enjoy. Let them do good, that they be rich in good works, ready to give, willing to share, storing up for themselves a good foundation for the time to come, that they may lay hold on eternal life.

1 Timothy 6:17-19, NKJV

There is that scattereth, and yet increaseth; and there is that withholdeth more than is meet, but it tendeth to poverty. The liberal soul shall be made fat: and he that watereth shall be watered also himself.

Proverbs 11:24-25, KJV

Whoever sows sparingly will also reap sparingly, and whoever sows generously will also reap generously. Each man should give what he has decided in his heart to give, not reluctantly or under compulsion, for God loves a cheerful giver. And God is able to make all grace abound to you, so that in all things at all times, having all that you need, you will abound in every good work. Now he who supplies seed to the sower and bread for food will also supply and increase your store of seed and will enlarge the harvest of your righteousness. You will be made rich in every way so that you can be generous on every occasion, and through us your generosity will result in thanksgiving to God.

2 Corinthians 9:6-8, 10-11, NIV

He that hath a bountiful eye shall be blessed; for he giveth of his bread to the poor.

Proverbs 22:9, KJV

"In everything I did, I showed you that by this kind of hard work we must help the weak, remembering the words the Lord Jesus himself said: 'It is more blessed to give than to receive.'"

Acts 20:35, NIV

"And if you lend to those from whom you expect to receive, what credit is that to you? Even sinners lend to sinners, to get back the same amount. But love your enemies, and do good, and lend, expecting nothing in return, and your reward will be great, and you will be sons of the Most High, for he is kind to the ungrateful and the evil. Give, and it will be given to you. Good measure, pressed down, shaken together, running over, will be put into your lap. For with the measure you use it will be measured back to you."

Luke 6:34-35, 38, ESV

"Give, and it will be given to you. Good measure, pressed down, shaken together, running over, will be put into your lap. For with the measure you use it will be measured back to you."

Luke 6:38, ESV

GRACE

Unto every one of us is given grace according to the measure of the gift of Christ.

Ephesians 4:7, KJV

Money cannot buy things like peace, tranquillity of mind, joy and fullness of life. These qualities have no price tags. They are God's gifts of grace which are freely available to rich and poor.

Everything we enjoy that is good and worthwhile, we enjoy by the grace of God. We don't deserve these things, we cannot earn them and we are not worthy of them. We are who we are and have what we have because of Christ's unfathomable love and grace toward us. This love compelled Him to sacrifice His life for us.

And for this very reason you should never take for granted the blessings which you receive from His hand. Always remember that they are gifts of God's endless goodness and a sign of His love for you.

GRACE
FROM GOD

For the LORD God is a sun and shield; the LORD will give grace and glory; no good thing will He withhold from those who walk uprightly.

Psalm 84:11, NKJV

And the Word became flesh and dwelt among us, and we have seen his glory, glory as of the only Son from the Father, full of grace and truth. And from his fullness we have all received, grace upon grace. For the law was given through Moses; grace and truth came through Jesus Christ.

John 1:14, 16-17, ESV

For by grace you have been saved through faith, and that not of yourselves; it is the gift of God, not of works, lest anyone should boast. For we are His workmanship, created in Christ Jesus for good works, which God prepared beforehand that we should walk in them.

Ephesians 2:8-10, NKJV

For you know the grace of our Lord Jesus Christ, that though he was rich, yet for your sake he became poor, so that you by his poverty might become rich.

2 Corinthians. 8:9, ESV

But he giveth more grace. Wherefore he saith, God resisteth the proud, but giveth grace unto the humble.

James 4:6, KJV

Sin shall not be your master, because you are not under law, but under grace.

Romans 6:14, NIV

"So now, brethren, I commend you to God and to the word of His grace, which is able to build you up and give you an inheritance among all those who are sanctified."

Acts 20:32, NKJV

Let us therefore come boldly unto the throne of grace, that we may obtain mercy, and find grace to help in time of need.

Hebrews 4:16, KJV

But he said to me, "My grace is sufficient for you, for my power is made perfect in weakness."

2 Corinthians 12:9, NIV

Therefore being justified by faith, we have peace with God through our Lord Jesus Christ: By whom also we have access by faith into this grace wherein we stand, and rejoice in hope of the glory of God.

Romans 5:1-2, KJV

But by the grace of God I am what I am, and his grace toward me was not in vain. On the contrary, I worked harder than any of them, though it was not I, but the grace of God that is with me.

1 Corinthians 15:10, ESV

The grace of the Lord Jesus Christ, and the love of God, and the communion of the Holy Spirit be with you all. Amen.

2 Corinthians 13:14, NKJV

GRATITUDE

Oh, give thanks to the LORD, for He is good! For His mercy endures forever.

Psalm 107:1, NKJV

In the hustle and bustle of everyday life, it is easy to forget about ordinary courtesy. Because people are being paid for the service that they render, we forget that a word of appreciation could change their duty into a blessing.

The habit of saying "Thank you" enriches every aspect of our lives. It costs nothing, but creates so much joy for both the giver and the receiver. Always be ready to express thanks. You will then discover how much joy you can bring to others.

If this is true on an ordinary human level, how much more should we express gratitude toward our Heavenly Father. All that we have, He gave to us, and we so seldom say thank You to Him. When we indeed do it, our spirit is set free and we experience a joy and blessing that could only come from God.

THE WORD'S VIEW

ON GRATITUDE

Let us come before his presence with thanksgiving, and make a joyful noise unto him with psalms.

Psalm 95:2, KJV

I urge, then, first of all, that requests, prayers, intercession and thanksgiving be made for everyone – for kings and all those in authority, that we may live peaceful and quiet lives in all godliness and holiness.

1 Timothy 2:1-2, NIV

And whatsoever ye do in word or deed, do all in the name of the Lord Jesus, giving thanks to God and the Father by him.

Colossians 3:17, KJV

Enter his gates with thanksgiving, and his courts with praise! Give thanks to him; bless his name!

Psalm 100:4, ESV

Sing unto the LORD with thanksgiving; sing praise upon the harp unto our God.

Psalm 147:7, KJV

Therefore, since we are receiving a kingdom that cannot be shaken, let us be thankful, and so worship God acceptably with reverence and awe, for our God is a consuming fire.

Hebrews 12:28-29, NIV

In every thing give thanks: for this is the will of God in Christ Jesus concerning you.

1 Thessalonians 5:18, KJV

Let there be no filthiness nor foolish talk nor crude joking, which are out of place, but instead let there be thanksgiving.

Ephesians 5:4, ESV

All this is for your benefit, so that the grace that is reaching more and more people may cause thanksgiving to overflow to the glory of God.

2 Corinthians 4:15, NIV

But thanks be to God, who gives us the victory through our Lord Jesus Christ.

1 Corinthians 15:57, ESV

Oh, give thanks to the LORD! Call upon His name; make known His deeds among the peoples!

1 Chronicles 16:8, NKJV

May you be strengthened with all power, according to his glorious might, for all endurance and patience with joy, giving thanks to the Father, who has qualified you to share in the inheritance of the saints in light.

Colossians 1:11-12, ESV

Through Jesus, therefore, let us continually offer to God a sacrifice of praise – the fruit of lips that confess his name.

Hebrews 13:15, NIV

Thy words were found, and I did eat them; and thy word was unto me the joy and rejoicing of mine heart: for I am called by thy name, O LORD God of hosts.

Jeremiah 15:16, KJV

Both riches and honor come from You, and You reign over all. In Your hand is power and might; in Your hand it is to make great and to give strength to all. Now therefore, our God, we thank You and praise Your glorious name.

1 Chronicles 29:12-13, NKJV

GUIDANCE

Thou shalt guide me with thy counsel, and afterward receive me to glory.

Psalm 73:24, KJV

There are certain guidelines that apply to all Christians wishing to find the will of God for their lives. The call to sanctification, to spiritual growth, to love and serve your fellow man, are just a few commands that apply to all those who love and serve Jesus Christ. But when your Christianity becomes a personal experience you come face to face with the question: "Lord, what do You want of *me*?" If God has a specific task for you, He will guide you on His way and accompany you. As you become aware of His guidance, you will become enthusiastic about the work that He has entrusted to you.

This enthusiasm is important in your prayers; it will help you to discern the will of God. In this way you will be inspired by new, creative ideas and methods for effective service. Keep your thoughts open and your spirit receptive to the work of God's Holy Spirit.

GUIDANCE FROM
THE WORD

I will instruct you and teach you in the way you should go; I will guide you with My eye.

Psalm 32:8, NKJV

In all thy ways acknowledge him, and he shall direct thy paths.

Proverbs 3:6, KJV

The steps of a man are established by the LORD, when he delights in his way; though he fall, he shall not be cast headlong, for the LORD upholds his hand.

Psalm 37:23-24, ESV

Whether you turn to the right or to the left, your ears will hear a voice behind you, saying, "This is the way; walk in it."

Isaiah 30:21, NIV

The LORD will guide you always; he will satisfy your needs in a sun-scorched land and will strengthen your frame. You will be like a well-watered garden, like a spring whose waters never fail.

Isaiah 58:11, NIV

Teach me to do your will, for you are my God; may your good Spirit lead me on level ground.

Psalm 143:10, NIV

Show me Your ways, O LORD; teach me Your paths. Lead me in Your truth and teach me, for You are the God of my salvation; on You I wait all the day.

Psalm 25:4-5, NKJV

"When the Spirit of truth comes, he will guide you into all the truth, for he will not speak on his own authority, but whatever he hears he will speak, and he will declare to you the things that are to come."

John 16:13, ESV

Let the word of Christ dwell in you richly in all wisdom, teaching and admonishing one another in psalms and hymns and spiritual songs, singing with grace in your hearts to the Lord.

Colossians 3:16, NKJV

Wherewithal shall a young man cleanse his way? by taking heed thereto according to thy word.

Psalm 119:9, KJV

Thy word is a lamp unto my feet, and a light unto my path.

Psalm 119:105, KJV

By day the LORD went ahead of them in a pillar of cloud to guide them on their way and by night in a pillar of fire to give them light, so that they could travel by day or night.

Exodus 13:21, NIV

For you are my rock and my fortress; and for your name's sake you lead me and guide me.

Psalm 31:3, ESV

I will give you shepherds after my own heart, who will lead you with knowledge and understanding.

Jeremiah 3:15, NIV

He leads the humble in what is right, and teaches the humble his way.

Psalm 25:9, ESV

O send out thy light and thy truth: let them lead me; let them bring me unto thy holy hill, and to thy tabernacles.

Psalm 43:3, KJV

HOPE

For You are my hope, O Lord GOD; you are my trust from my youth.

Psalm 71:5, NKJV

In the Tate Gallery in London is a striking painting by Frederick Watts. The title of the painting is *Hope*. A beautiful woman is sitting, blindfolded, on top of a world globe and in her hand is a lute. All but one of the strings is broken. She touches that one string with her finger and leans forward to catch its sound. She is filled with *hope* – believing the best in the worst circumstances.

As long as Christian hope is alive, life cannot break us, we will not snap under the weight of our problems and afflictions. We know that God is able to make the best out of the worst.

Where Christian hope exists, no night can be completely dark, no loneliness is without comfort, and no fear overwhelming. Christian hope is based on God's omnipotence. It is faith that fills a heart with joy even when it is on the verge of breaking. Hope gives us an invincible spirit.

THE WORD'S VIEW

ON HOPE

Therefore, preparing your minds for action, and being sober-minded, set your hope fully on the grace that will be brought to you at the revelation of Jesus Christ.

1 Peter 1:13, ESV

Behold, the eye of the LORD is upon them that fear him, upon them that hope in his mercy; To deliver their soul from death, and to keep them alive in famine.

Psalm 33:18-19, KJV

Why are you downcast, O my soul? Why so disturbed within me? Put your hope in God, for I will yet praise him, my Savior and my God.

Psalm 42:5-6, NIV

Now may our Lord Jesus Christ himself, and God our Father, who loved us and gave us eternal comfort and good hope through grace, comfort your hearts and establish them in every good work and word.

2 Thessalonians 2:16-17, ESV

This I recall to my mind, therefore have I hope. The LORD is my portion, saith my soul; therefore will I hope in him. The LORD is good unto them that wait for him, to the soul that seeketh him. It is good that a man should both hope and quietly wait for the salvation of the LORD.

Lamentations 3:21, 24-26, KJV

Even youths grow tired and weary, and young men stumble and fall; but those who hope in the LORD will renew their strength.

Isaiah 40:30-31, NIV

For to this end we toil and strive, because we have our hope set on the living God, who is the Savior of all people, especially of those who believe.

1 Timothy 4:10, ESV

Therefore did my heart rejoice, and my tongue was glad; moreover also my flesh shall rest in hope: Because thou wilt not leave my soul in hell, neither wilt thou suffer thine Holy One to see corruption.

Acts 2:26-27, KJV

And we rejoice in the hope of the glory of God. Not only so, but we also rejoice in our sufferings, because we know that suffering produces perseverance; perseverance, character; and character, hope. And hope does not disappoint us, because God has poured out his love into our hearts by the Holy Spirit, whom he has given us.

Romans 5:2-5, NIV

Know that wisdom is such to your soul; if you find it, there will be a future, and your hope will not be cut off.

Proverbs 24:14, ESV

We have this hope as an anchor for the soul, firm and secure.

Hebrews 6:19, NIV

Now may the God of hope fill you with all joy and peace in believing, that you may abound in hope by the power of the Holy Spirit.

Romans 15:13, NKJV

Through him you believe in God, who raised him from the dead and glorified him, and so your faith and hope are in God.

1 Peter 1:21, NIV

ℋUMILITY

"Whoever exalts himself will be humbled, and whoever humbles himself will be exalted."

Matthew 23:12, ESV

The highest lesson a believer has to learn is humility. Oh, that every Christian who seeks to advance in holiness may remember this well! The highest holiness is the deepest humility. It does not come by itself, but only as it is made a matter of special dealing on the part of our faithful Lord.

It is indeed blessed to be so free from self that whatever is said about us or done to us is lost and swallowed up on the thought that Jesus is all. He watches over us with a jealous, loving care.

In trial and weakness and trouble, He seeks to bring us low, until we learn that His grace is all, and to take pleasure in the very thing that brings us and keeps us low. His strength made perfect in our weakness, His presence filling and satisfying our emptiness, becomes the secret of a humility that need never fail.

Promises for

The Humble

By humility and the fear of the LORD are riches and honor and life.

Proverbs 22:4, NKJV

Humble yourselves, therefore, under the mighty hand of God so that at the proper time he may exalt you.

1 Peter 5:6, ESV

For thus saith the high and lofty One that inhabiteth eternity, whose name is Holy; I dwell in the high and holy place, with him also that is of a contrite and humble spirit, to revive the spirit of the humble, and to revive the heart of the contrite ones.

Isaiah 57:15, KJV

"Blessed are the meek, for they will inherit the earth."

Matthew 5:5, NIV

Seek the LORD, all you humble of the land, who do his just commands; seek righteousness; seek humility; perhaps you may be hidden on the day of the anger of the LORD.

Zephaniah 2:3, ESV

"Assuredly, I say to you, unless you are converted and become as little children, you will by no means enter the kingdom of heaven. Therefore whoever humbles himself as this little child is the greatest in the kingdom of heaven."

Matthew 18:3-4, NKJV

Do not let your adornment be merely outward – arranging the hair, wearing gold, or putting on fine apparel – rather let it be the hidden person of the heart, with the incorruptible beauty of a gentle and quiet spirit, which is very precious in the sight of God.

1 Peter 3:3-4, NKJV

If my people, who are called by my name, will humble themselves and pray and seek my face and turn from their wicked ways, then will I hear from heaven and will forgive their sin and will heal their land.

2 Chronicles 7:14, NIV

Let another praise you, and not your own mouth; someone else, and not your own lips.

Proverbs 27:2, NIV

"If anyone would be first, he must be last of all and servant of all."

Mark 9:35, ESV

The lofty looks of man shall be humbled, and the haughtiness of men shall be bowed down, and the LORD alone shall be exalted in that day.

Isaiah 2:11, KJV

A man's pride will bring him low, but the humble in spirit will retain honor.

Proverbs 29:23, NKJV

Let nothing be done through strife or vainglory; but in lowliness of mind let each esteem other better than themselves. Look not every man on his own things, but every man also on the things of others. Let this mind be in you, which was also in Christ Jesus: Who, being in the form of God, thought it not robbery to be equal with God: But made himself of no reputation, and took upon him the form of a servant, and was made in the likeness of men: And being found in fashion as a man, he humbled himself, and became obedient unto death, even the death of the cross. Wherefore God also hath highly exalted him, and given him a name which is above every name.

Philippians 2:3-9, KJV

JEALOUSY

A tranquil heart gives life to the flesh, but envy makes the bones rot.

Proverbs 14:30, ESV

Material possessions have become the standard that measures success in our world. And we fall into the trap so easily, believing that if we only had more, bigger, better, then we would be happy. But the Bible warns us not to base our happiness on uncertain riches. We should be content with what we have, not coveting what others have.

True riches are not measured by the accumulation of wealth, but by what is stored in the heart. When you are tempted to complain about your lack, and your neighbor's gain, stop and count the blessings that God pours out on you day by day. And soon you'll see that others will envy you for the peace, joy and love that fills your life.

THE WORD'S RESPONSE

TO JEALOUSY

Now godliness with contentment is great gain. For we brought nothing into this world, and it is certain we can carry nothing out. And having food and clothing, with these we shall be content.

1 Timothy 6:6-8, NKJV

Those who belong to Christ Jesus have crucified the sinful nature with its passions and desires. Since we live by the Spirit, let us keep in step with the Spirit. Let us not become conceited, provoking and envying each other.

Galatians 5:24-26, NIV

Let us walk honestly, as in the day; not in rioting and drunkenness, not in chambering and wantonness, not in strife and envying.

Romans 13:13, KJV

And I saw that all labor and all achievement spring from man's envy of his neighbor. This too is meaningless, a chasing after the wind.

Ecclesiastes 4:4, NIV

But if you have bitter envy and self-seeking in your hearts, do not boast and lie against the truth. This wisdom does not descend from above, but is earthly, sensual, demonic. For where envy and self-seeking exist, confusion and every evil thing are there.

James 3:14-16, NKJV

Wrath is cruel and anger a torrent, but who is able to stand before jealousy?

Proverbs 27:4, NKJV

Let no one seek his own good, but the good of his neighbor.

1 Corinthians 10:24, ESV

Keep your lives free from the love of money and be content with what you have.

Hebrews 13:5, NIV

For wrath killeth the foolish man, and envy slayeth the silly one.

Job 5:2, KJV

Do not envy the oppressor, and choose none of his ways.

Proverbs 3:31, NKJV

Let not your heart envy sinners, but continue in the fear of the LORD all the day.

Proverbs 23:17, ESV

Do not fret because of evildoers, nor be envious of the workers of iniquity.

Psalm 37:1, NKJV

Now the works of the flesh are evident: sexual immorality, impurity, sensuality, idolatry, sorcery, enmity, strife, jealousy, fits of anger, rivalries, dissensions, divisions, envy, drunkenness, orgies, and things like these. I warn you, as I warned you before, that those who do such things will not inherit the kingdom of God.

Galatians 5:19-21, ESV

Therefore, rid yourselves of all malice and all deceit, hypocrisy, envy, and slander of every kind.

1 Peter 2:1, NIV

Love is patient and kind; love does not envy or boast; it is not arrogant.

1 Corinthians 13:4, ESV

Joy

Rejoice in the Lord always. I will say it again: Rejoice!

> Philippians 4:4, NIV

The hallmark of a Christian's life should be the joy with which he approaches each new day. No matter how difficult the circumstances in which we find ourselves, we carry in our hearts the presence of God. And in the presence of God there is fullness of joy. This joy is based in the knowledge that God is good and God is in control, and all things will work out for our good, as we love Him and walk in His purpose for our lives. It is a joy that the world finds difficult to understand, because their joy is circumstantial.

As we grow in Christ, we find that the fruit of the Holy Spirit increases in us. Our perspective on events changes, and we are able to see in each circumstance a glimpse of the joy that comes from the presence of God.

THE JOY
OF THE LORD

He will yet fill your mouth with laughter
and your lips with shouts of joy.

Job 8:21, NIV

"You now have sorrow; but I will see you
again and your heart will rejoice, and your
joy no one will take from you. Until now
you have asked nothing in My name. Ask,
and you will receive, that your joy may be
full."

John 16:22, 24, NKJV

But I have trusted in your steadfast love;
my heart shall rejoice in your salvation. I
will sing to the LORD, because he has dealt
bountifully with me.

Psalm 13:5-6, ESV

Thou wilt shew me the path of life: in thy
presence is fulness of joy; at thy right hand
there are pleasures for evermore.

Psalm 16:11, KJV

The joy of the LORD is your strength.

Nehemiah 8:10, ESV

Though you have not seen him, you love him; and even though you do not see him now, you believe in him and are filled with an inexpressible and glorious joy, for you are receiving the goal of your faith, the salvation of your souls.

1 Peter 1:8-9, NIV

Those who sow in tears will reap with songs of joy. He who goes out weeping, carrying seed to sow, will return with songs of joy, carrying sheaves with him.

Psalm 126:5-6, NIV

For you shall go out in joy and be led forth in peace; the mountains and the hills before you shall break forth into singing, and all the trees of the field shall clap their hands.

Isaiah 55:12, ESV

A merry heart maketh a cheerful countenance: but by sorrow of the heart the spirit is broken.

Proverbs 15:13, KJV

Yet I will rejoice in the LORD, I will joy in the God of my salvation.

Habakkuk 3:18, NKJV

JOY

We also rejoice in God through our Lord Jesus Christ, through whom we have now received reconciliation.

Romans 5:11, NIV

This is the day that the LORD has made; let us rejoice and be glad in it.

Psalm 118:24, ESV

For the kingdom of God is not meat and drink; but righteousness, and peace, and joy in the Holy Ghost.

Romans 14:17, KJV

But the fruit of the Spirit is love, joy, peace, patience, kindness, goodness, faithfulness, gentleness and self-control.

Galatians 5:22-23, NIV

Therefore with joy shall ye draw water out of the wells of salvation.

Isaiah 12:3, KJV

The ransomed of the LORD shall return, and come to Zion with singing, with everlasting joy on their heads. They shall obtain joy and gladness; sorrow and sighing shall flee away.

Isaiah 51:11, NKJV

*L*OVE OF GOD

Your love, O LORD, reaches to the heavens, your
faithfulness to the skies.

Psalm 36:5, NIV

The reason and motive of our salvation lies
in the loving nature of God. It is not a case
of our loving God but of His loving us and
giving His Son for our redemption. We love
God only because He first loved us, and He
loved us so, so greatly, so very much. There
is no god in the universe whose nature is
love or who so displays his mercy. Other
gods are to be dreaded and appeased; their
nature is unpredictable and their wrath is
cruel. But this God, the God and Father of
our Lord Jesus Christ, is our God and our
Father, bless His name.

In His love He delivered us from both
the power and guilt of our sins and from
the eternal judgment to which we were
hastening. With His strong cords of love
He drew us out, and then He washed us and
set us on our way.

Assurance of
God's love

For I am persuaded that neither death nor life, nor angels nor principalities nor powers, nor things present nor things to come, nor height nor depth, nor any other created thing, shall be able to separate us from the love of God which is in Christ Jesus our Lord.

Romans 8:38-39, NKJV

See what kind of love the Father has given to us, that we should be called children of God; and so we are.

1 John 3:1, ESV

And we have known and believed the love that God hath to us. God is love; and he that dwelleth in love dwelleth in God, and God in him.

1 John 4:16, KJV

But God, being rich in mercy, because of the great love with which he loved us, even when we were dead in our trespasses, made us alive together with Christ.

Ephesians 2:4-5, ESV

"The Father Himself loves you, because you have loved Me, and have believed that I came forth from God."

John 16:27, NKJV

The LORD hath appeared of old unto me, saying, Yea, I have loved thee with an everlasting love: therefore with lovingkindness have I drawn thee.

Jeremiah 31:3, KJV

"I made known to them your name, and I will continue to make it known, that the love with which you have loved me may be in them, and I in them."

John 17:26, ESV

And he will love thee, and bless thee, and multiply thee: he will also bless the fruit of thy womb, and the fruit of thy land, thy corn, and thy wine, and thine oil, the increase of thy kine, and the flocks of thy sheep, in the land which he sware unto thy fathers to give thee.

Deuteronomy 7:13, KJV

"As the Father hath loved me, so have I loved you: continue ye in my love."

John 15:9, KJV

May the Lord direct your hearts into the love of God and into the patience of Christ.

2 Thessalonians 3:5, NKJV

In this the love of God was made manifest among us, that God sent his only Son into the world, so that we might live through him. In this is love, not that we have loved God but that he loved us and sent his Son to be the propitiation for our sins.

1 John 4:9-10, ESV

"For God so loved the world that he gave his one and only Son, that whoever believes in him shall not perish but have eternal life."

John 3:16, NIV

Wondrously show your steadfast love, O Savior of those who seek refuge from their adversaries at your right hand.

Psalm 17:7, ESV

[I pray] that you, being rooted and grounded in love, may be able to comprehend with all the saints what is the width and length and depth and height – to know the love of Christ which passes knowledge; that you may be filled with all the fullness of God.

Ephesians 3:17-19, NKJV

LOVE OF OTHERS

Beloved, if God so loved us, we ought also to love one another.

1 John 4:11, KJV

People are particularly interesting beings. They differ so radically from each other that life among them will never be monotonous. It is an irrefutable fact that your attitude toward people will determine their attitude toward you.

If you are constantly criticizing your fellowmen, you erect a barrier that the spirit of friendship finds hard to overcome. If you regard others with contempt, you will soon taste the bitter fruit of loneliness.

Your attitude toward others should be inspired by the Holy Spirit and motivated by the attitude of Jesus Christ. The most constructive way to live, is to love people. Bitterness vanishes, shyness is overcome and inferiority is replaced by self-confidence. The voluntary giving of your love does not only enrich your own life, but will draw people to you who will enhance your quality of life.

ENCOURAGEMENT

TO LOVE OTHERS

Beloved, let us love one another, for love is of God; and everyone who loves is born of God and knows God. He who does not love does not know God, for God is love.

1 John 4:7-8, NKJV

And this is my prayer: that your love may abound more and more in knowledge and depth of insight, so that you may be able to discern what is best and may be pure and blameless until the day of Christ.

Philippians 1:9-10, NIV

He that loveth his brother abideth in the light, and there is none occasion of stumbling in him.

1 John 2:10, KJV

Let love be without hypocrisy. Abhor what is evil. Cling to what is good. Be kindly affectionate to one another with brotherly love, in honor giving preference to one another; not lagging in diligence, fervent in spirit, serving the Lord.

Romans 12:9-11, NKJV

"A new commandment I give to you, that you love one another; as I have loved you, that you also love one another. By this all will know that you are My disciples, if you have love for one another."

John 13:34-35, NKJV

And may the Lord make you increase and abound in love for one another and for all, as we do for you, so that he may establish your hearts blameless in holiness before our God and Father, at the coming of our Lord Jesus with all his saints.

1 Thessalonians 3:12-13, ESV

Above all, keep loving one another earnestly, since love covers a multitude of sins.

1 Peter 4:8, ESV

Seeing ye have purified your souls in obeying the truth through the Spirit unto unfeigned love of the brethren, see that ye love one another with a pure heart fervently.

1 Peter 1:22, KJV

My little children, let us not love in word or in tongue, but in deed and in truth.

1 John 3:18, NKJV

"Love your neighbor as yourself."

Luke 10:27, NIV

Now concerning brotherly love you have no need for anyone to write to you, for you yourselves have been taught by God to love one another.

1 Thessalonians 4:9, ESV

"But I say unto you, Love your enemies, bless them that curse you, do good to them that hate you, and pray for them which despitefully use you, and persecute you; That ye may be the children of your Father which is in heaven: for he maketh his sun to rise on the evil and on the good, and sendeth rain on the just and on the unjust. For if ye love them which love you, what reward have ye? do not even the publicans the same?"

Matthew 5:44-46, KJV

Keep on loving each other as brothers. Do not forget to entertain strangers, for by so doing some people have entertained angels without knowing it. Remember those in prison as if you were their fellow prisoners, and those who are mistreated as if you yourselves were suffering.

Hebrews 13:1-3, NIV

LOVING GOD

Thou shalt love the Lord thy God with all thy heart, and with all thy soul, and with all thy strength, and with all thy mind; and thy neighbour as thyself.

Luke 10:27, KJV

It is easy to love someone who has been good to you – and God has been better than the best toward us. He has saved us, and protected us, and provided for our every need. He demonstrated His love by sending Jesus to die for us. God's love for us is an extravagant love, one that gives all He has and all He is. And our love in return should be as passionate and heartfelt.

We should love God from the depth of our emotions, with every thought we think, with every decision of the will we make, with every action that we take. With our whole heart, mind, soul, and strength. Our whole life should be an outpouring of the love we have for Him.

Promises for those
who love God

I love you, O Lord, my strength.

Psalm 18:1, ESV

"If anyone loves me, he will obey my teaching.
My Father will love him, and we will come
to him and make our home with him."

John 14:23, NIV

I love them that love me; and those that
seek me early shall find me.

Proverbs 8:17, KJV

Know therefore that the Lord your God
is God; he is the faithful God, keeping his
covenant of love to a thousand generations
of those who love him and keep his commands.

Deuteronomy 7:9, NIV

However, as it is written: "No eye has seen,
no ear has heard, no mind has conceived
what God has prepared for those who love
him" but God has revealed it to us by his
Spirit.

1 Corinthians 2:9-10, NIV

The LORD preserves all who love him, but all the wicked he will destroy.

Psalm 145:20, ESV

I the LORD thy God am a jealous God, visiting the iniquity of the fathers upon the children unto the third and fourth generation of them that hate me; And shewing mercy unto thousands of them that love me, and keep my commandments.

Exodus 20:5-6, KJV

Because he hath set his love upon me, therefore will I deliver him: I will set him on high, because he hath known my name.

Psalm 91:14, KJV

So if you faithfully obey the commands I am giving you today – to love the LORD your God and to serve him with all your heart and with all your soul – then I will send rain on your land in its season, both autumn and spring rains, so that you may gather in your grain, new wine and oil.

Deuteronomy 11:13-14, NIV

O you who love the LORD, hate evil!

Psalm 97:10, ESV

I love the LORD, for he heard my voice; he heard my cry for mercy.

Psalm 116:1, NIV

We love him, because he first loved us.

1 John 4:19, KJV

Love the LORD, all his saints! The LORD preserves the faithful, but the proud he pays back in full.

Psalm 31:23, NIV

Though you have not seen him, you love him. Though you do not now see him, you believe in him and rejoice with joy that is inexpressible and filled with glory.

1 Peter 1:8, ESV

And now, Israel, what does the LORD your God require of you, but to fear the LORD your God, to walk in all His ways and to love Him, to serve the LORD your God with all your heart and with all your soul, and to keep the commandments of the Lord.

Deuteronomy 10:12-13, NKJV

*L*YING

Whoever would love life and see good days must keep his tongue from evil and his lips from deceitful speech.

1 *Peter* 3:10, NIV

Lies cause loveless rifts between people, but truthful words build bridges between them. When you care about others, you are enfolded by their love. But when you tell lies about them because you do not like them, everything starts to collapse.

To rejoice in the truth is not always that easy. There are times when we really do not want the truth to triumph. Then there are also times when the truth is the last thing we want to hear. Christian love has no need for concealing the truth: it is courageous enough to listen to the truth and to deal with it. It has nothing to hide and finds happiness in the fact that truth *will* prevail. Love makes it possible to hear the truth without fear.

The Word's view

on lying

The lip of truth shall be established for ever: but a lying tongue is but for a moment.

Proverbs 12:19, KJV

Lying lips are an abomination to the LORD, but those who act faithfully are his delight.

Proverbs 12:22, ESV

Therefore, putting away lying, "Let each one of you speak truth with his neighbor," for we are members of one another.

Ephesians 4:25, NKJV

Do not lie to each other, since you have taken off your old self with its practices and have put on the new self, which is being renewed in knowledge in the image of its Creator.

Colossians 3:9-10, NIV

The integrity of the upright shall guide them: but the perverseness of transgressors shall destroy them.

Proverbs 11:3, KJV

Put away perversity from your mouth; keep corrupt talk far from your lips.

Proverbs 4:24, NIV

The heart of the wise makes his speech judicious and adds persuasiveness to his lips. Gracious words are like a honeycomb, sweetness to the soul and health to the body.

Proverbs 16:23-24, ESV

Deliver my soul, O LORD, from lying lips, and from a deceitful tongue.

Psalm 120:2, KJV

The one who conceals hatred has lying lips, and whoever utters slander is a fool. When words are many, transgression is not lacking, but whoever restrains his lips is prudent.

Proverbs 10:18-19, ESV

Whoever of you loves life and desires to see many good days, keep your tongue from evil and your lips from speaking lies.

Psalm 34:12-13, NIV

A man who bears false witness against his neighbor is like a war club, or a sword, or a sharp arrow.

Proverbs 25:18, ESV

You shall not go about as a talebearer among your people; nor shall you take a stand against the life of your neighbor: I am the LORD.

Leviticus 19:16, NKJV

He that goeth about as a talebearer revealeth secrets: therefore meddle not with him that flattereth with his lips.

Proverbs 20:19, KJV

If a false witness rises against any man to testify against him of wrongdoing, then both men in the controversy shall stand before the Lord, before the priests and the judges who serve in those days. And the judges shall make careful inquiry, and, if the witness is a false witness, who has testified falsely against his brother, then you shall do to him as he thought to have done to his brother; so you shall put away the evil from among you.

Deuteronomy 19:16-19, NKJV

"Speak the truth to each other, and render true and sound judgment in your courts; do not plot evil against your neighbor, and do not love to swear falsely. I hate all this," declares the LORD.

Zechariah 8:16-17, NIV

MARRIAGE

The LORD God said, It is not good that the man should be alone; I will make him an help meet for him.
Genesis 2:18, KJV

One of the saddest aspects of society is the insignificant regard that many people have for the sanctity of marriage. Faithfulness in marriage is valued so lightly that it often seems to be the exception rather than the rule. Divorce is taking on epidemic proportions. Countless people do not marry but live together raising families out of wedlock. Many people compromise in marriage, relegating the marriage contract to "a small piece of paper." Many of these problems stem from the refusal to accept responsibility. No marriage can last without the touch of God's grace that enables two people to keep seemingly super-human vows to each other and to God.

God insituted the holy ordinance of marriage. A man and a woman make a covenant before Him in which they promise to live faithfully before Him, to build a family, and to face life's joys and problems together.

THE WORD'S VIEW

ON MARRIAGE

They asked, "Is it lawful for a man to divorce his wife for any and every reason?" "Haven't you read," he replied, "that at the beginning the Creator 'made them male and female,' and said, 'For this reason a man will leave his father and mother and be united to his wife, and the two will become one flesh'? So they are no longer two, but one. Therefore what God has joined together, let man not separate."

Matthew 19:3-6, NIV

Let your fountain be blessed, and rejoice with the wife of your youth. As a loving deer and a graceful doe, let her breasts satisfy you at all times; and always be enraptured with her love.

Proverbs 5:18-19, NKJV

Wives, submit to your husbands as to the Lord. For the husband is the head of the wife as Christ is the head of the church, his body, of which he is the Savior.

Ephesians 5:22-23, NIV

He who finds a wife finds a good thing and obtains favor from the LORD.

Proverbs 18:22, ESV

House and riches are the inheritance of fathers and a prudent wife is from the LORD.

Proverbs 19:14, KJV

Two are better than one, because they have a good return for their work. Also, if two lie down together, they will keep warm. But how can one keep warm alone?

Ecclesiastes 4:9, 11, NIV

Husbands, love your wives, just as Christ loved the church and gave himself up for her.

Ephesians 5:25, NIV

In this same way, husbands ought to love their wives as their own bodies. He who loves his wife loves himself.

Ephesians 5:28, NIV

However, each one of you also must love his wife as he loves himself, and the wife must respect her husband.

Ephesians 5:33, NIV

I am my beloved's, and his desire is for me.

Song of Songs 7:10, ESV

Love suffers long and is kind; love does not envy; love does not parade itself, is not puffed up; does not behave rudely, does not seek its own, is not provoked, thinks no evil; does not rejoice in iniquity, but rejoices in the truth; bears all things, believes all things, hopes all things, endures all things. Love never fails.

1 Corinthians 13:4-8, NKJV

Who can find a virtuous woman? for her price is far above rubies. The heart of her husband doth safely trust in her, so that he shall have no need of spoil. Her children arise up, and call her blessed; her husband also, and he praiseth her.

Proverbs 31:10-11, 28, KJV

Let the husband render to his wife the affection due her, and likewise also the wife to her husband. The wife does not have authority over her own body, but the husband does. And likewise the husband does not have authority over his own body, but the wife does.

1 Corinthians 7:3-4, NKJV

$\mathcal{M}$ONEY

But my God shall supply all your need according to his riches in glory by Christ Jesus.
Philippians 4:19, KJV

Money can become a blessing or a curse, depending on the priority it has in your life. It is tragic when the acquiring of great wealth becomes the driving force in a person's life. When money is an idol it becomes so demanding that it destroys everything that is beautiful and worthwhile in one's character.

If money is kept in the right place in our life and if it remains a servant, it can be a great blessing. It might make life more comfortable, but there are qualities that come without a price tag and that are essential for true life.

We have to remind ourselves constantly that money can buy books, but not intellect; a bed, but not peaceful sleep; food, but not appetite; entertainment, but not happiness; luxuries, but not culture; a Bible, but not heaven. People often forget that the most valuable things in life are free.

The Word's view

ON MONEY

In the day of prosperity be joyful, but in the day of adversity consider: Surely God has appointed the one as well as the other, so that man can find out nothing that will come after him.

Ecclesiastes 7:14, NKJV

"But when you give to the needy, do not let your left hand know what your right hand is doing, so that your giving may be in secret. And your Father who sees in secret will reward you."

Matthew 6:3-4, ESV

I have been young, and now am old; yet have I not seen the righteous forsaken, nor his seed begging bread. He is ever merciful, and lendeth; and his seed is blessed.

Psalm 37:25-26, KJV

But just as you excel in everything – in faith, in speech, in knowledge, in complete earnestness and in your love for us – see that you also excel in this grace of giving.

2 Corinthians 8:7, NIV

"Give, and it will be given to you. A good measure, pressed down, shaken together and running over, will be poured into your lap. For with the measure you use, it will be measured to you."

Luke 6:38, NIV

Now there is great gain in godliness with contentment, for we brought nothing into the world, and we cannot take anything out of the world. But if we have food and clothing, with these we will be content. But those who desire to be rich fall into temptation, into a snare, into many senseless and harmful desires that plunge people into ruin and destruction. For the love of money is a root of all kinds of evils. It is through this craving that some have wandered away from the faith and pierced themselves with many pangs.

1 Timothy 6:6-10, ESV

"Bring the whole tithe into the storehouse, that there may be food in my house. Test me in this," says the LORD Almighty, "and see if I will not throw open the floodgates of heaven and pour out so much blessing that you will not have room enough for it."

Malachi 3:10, NIV

Give me neither poverty nor riches – feed me with the food allotted to me; lest I be full and deny You, and say, "Who is the LORD?" Or lest I be poor and steal, and profane the name of my God.

Proverbs 30:8-9, NKJV

Love not the world, neither the things that are in the world. If any man love the world, the love of the Father is not in him. For all that is in the world, the lust of the flesh, and the lust of the eyes, and the pride of life, is not of the Father, but is of the world. And the world passeth away, and the lust thereof: but he that doeth the will of God abideth for ever.

1 John 2:15-17, KJV

Moreover, when God gives any man wealth and possessions, and enables him to enjoy them, to accept his lot and be happy in his work – this is a gift of God.

Ecclesiastes 5:19, NIV

Naked came I out of my mother's womb, and naked shall I return thither: the LORD gave, and the LORD hath taken away; blessed be the name of the LORD.

Job 1:21, KJV

OBEDIENCE

"If you know these things, blessed are you if you do them."

John 13:17, NKJV

Many people experience their service to God as a heavy burden instead of pure joy. They feel that there are so many things that they have to lay down and that they enter into a life of hardship. They forget that a new life in Christ Jesus is a life of indescribable joy. When God asks us to lay down our old life, we can be confident that He will replace it with something much better.

Don't think that when God requires your total obedience, that your life will lose its joy. God finds it easier to use an obedient, happy person in His service than one who is overwhelmed by the thought of the heavy responsibility he believes it takes to serve the Lord.

If God has called you to a special responsibility, don't become so despondent that your life becomes a burden. Rejoice in the Lord and in His omnipotence and accept your duty with gladness and gratitude.

BLESSINGS

FOR OBEDIENCE

Hear therefore, O Israel, and observe to do it; that it may be well with thee, and that ye may increase mightily, as the LORD God of thy fathers hath promised thee, in the land that floweth with milk and honey.

Deuteronomy 6:3, KJV

"If you keep my commandments, you will abide in my love, just as I have kept my Father's commandments and abide in his love."

John 15:10, ESV

Do what is right and good in the LORD's sight, so that it may go well with you and you may go in and take over the good land that the LORD promised on oath to your forefathers.

Deuteronomy 6:18, NIV

"And because you listen to these rules and keep and do them, the Lord your God will keep with you the covenant and the steadfast love that he swore to your fathers."

Deuteronomy 7:12, ESV

Now therefore, if ye will obey my voice indeed, and keep my covenant, then ye shall be a peculiar treasure unto me above all people: for all the earth is mine.

Exodus 19:5, KJV

"Whosoever therefore shall break one of these least commandments, and shall teach men so, he shall be called the least in the kingdom of heaven: but whosoever shall do and teach them, the same shall be called great in the kingdom of heaven."

Matthew 5:19, KJV

Carefully follow the terms of this covenant, so that you may prosper in everything you do.

Deuteronomy 29:9, NIV

Beloved, if our heart does not condemn us, we have confidence before God; and whatever we ask we receive from him, because we keep his commandments and do what pleases him.

1 John 3:21-22, ESV

The things which you learned and received and heard and saw in me, these do, and the God of peace will be with you.

Philippians 4:9, NKJV

He openeth also their ear to discipline, and commandeth that they return from iniquity. If they obey and serve him, they shall spend their days in prosperity, and their years in pleasures.

Job 36:10-11, KJV

"See, I have set before you today life and good, death and evil, in that I command you today to love the LORD your God, to walk in His ways, and to keep His commandments, His statutes, and His judgments, that you may live and multiply; and the LORD your God will bless you in the land which you go to possess."

Deuteronomy 30:15-16, NKJV

And the world is passing away along with its desires, but whoever does the will of God abides forever.

1 John 2:17, ESV

But whoso looketh into the perfect law of liberty, and continueth therein, he being not a forgetful hearer, but a doer of the work, this man shall be blessed in his deed.

James 1:25, KJV

$\mathcal{P}$ATIENCE

Be still before the LORD and wait patiently for him.

Psalm 37:7, NIV

Impatience and impulsiveness are often the reasons for hasty decisions that are later regretted. It requires discipline and patience to accept God's will, to trust Him unconditionally and to submit to His will for your life. Many people insist that they need to make quick decisions and so do not lay matters before the Lord. They make rash decisions and follow their own instincts. But then they cannot escape the tension and worry that must inevitably follow. They can also not know if the decision they have made is the right one.

Jesus should be our example of One who, in spite of a busy life, put His trust totally in God the Father and waited on Him before He made any decisions, before He carried out any plans. He knew that in a demanding, fast-paced world, God's timing is always perfect.

THE WORD'S VIEW

ON PATIENCE

I waited patiently for the LORD; he inclined to me and heard my cry.

Psalm 40:1, ESV

It is good that a man should both hope and quietly wait for the salvation of the LORD.

Lamentations 3:26, KJV

I have learned the secret of being content in any and every situation, whether well fed or hungry, whether living in plenty or in want. I can do everything through him who gives me strength.

Philippians 4:12-13, NIV

But I have calmed and quieted my soul, like a weaned child with its mother; like a weaned child is my soul within me.

Psalm 131:2, ESV

Since you have kept my command to endure patiently, I will also keep you from the hour of trial that is going to come upon the whole world to test those who live on the earth.

Revelation 3:10, NIV

And let us not grow weary while doing good, for in due season we shall reap if we do not lose heart.

Galatians 6:9, NKJV

"He who stands firm to the end will be saved."

Matthew 24:13, NIV

For ye have need of patience, that, after ye have done the will of God, ye might receive the promise.

Hebrews 10:36, KJV

Put on then, as God's chosen ones, holy and beloved, compassion, kindness, humility, meekness, and patience, bearing with one another and, if one has a complaint against another, forgiving each other; as the Lord has forgiven you, so you also must forgive.

Colossians 3:12-13, ESV

Therefore be patient, brethren, until the coming of the Lord. See how the farmer waits for the precious fruit of the earth, waiting patiently for it until it receives the early and latter rain. You also be patient. Establish your hearts, for the coming of the Lord is at hand.

James 5:7-8, NKJV

The Lord is not slack concerning his promise, as some men count slackness; but is longsuffering toward us, not willing that any should perish, but that all should come to repentance.

2 Peter 3:9, KJV

We also rejoice in our sufferings, because we know that suffering produces perseverance; perseverance, character; and character, hope.

Romans 5:3-4, NIV

My brethren, count it all joy when you fall into various trials, knowing that the testing of your faith produces patience. But let patience have its perfect work, that you may be perfect and complete, lacking nothing.

James 1:2-4, NKJV

But if we hope for that we see not, then do we with patience wait for it.

Romans 8:25, KJV

However, for this reason I obtained mercy, that in me first Jesus Christ might show all longsuffering, as a pattern to those who are going to believe on Him for everlasting life.

1 Timothy 1:16, NKJV

$\mathcal{P}$EACE

"Peace I leave with you; my peace I give you."
John 14:27, NIV

God is a God of peace. Jesus Christ is the Prince of Peace. Jesus tells us that those who live to make peace will be called sons of God.

The condition of being a peacemaker is that you live in peace with God, with yourself and with your fellowman. Peace is one of the most glorious fruits of the Holy Spirit.

This peace does not come through escapism, but through wrestling with and triumphing over problems. The road to peace often passes through conflict.

Peacemakers are blessed, because they do God's work here on earth. They are blessed because they make the world a better place to live and work in. Many people are locked in a personal civil war. Fortunate are those who find inner peace, because their lives belong to God and they are at peace with God and with themselves.

THE PROMISE

OF PEACE

My people will live in peaceful dwelling places, in secure homes, in undisturbed places of rest.

Isaiah 32:18, NIV

And I will give peace in the land, and ye shall lie down, and none shall make you afraid: and I will rid evil beasts out of the land, neither shall the sword go through your land.

Leviticus 26:6, KJV

I will both lie down in peace, and sleep; For You alone, O LORD, make me dwell in safety.

Psalm 4:8, NKJV

Now the God of peace, that brought again from the dead our Lord Jesus, that great shepherd of the sheep, through the blood of the everlasting covenant, make you perfect in every good work to do his will, working in you that which is wellpleasing in his sight, through Jesus Christ; to whom be glory for ever and ever.

Hebrews 13:20-21, KJV

Be careful for nothing; but in every thing by prayer and supplication with thanksgiving let your requests be made known unto God. And the peace of God, which passeth all understanding, shall keep your hearts and minds through Christ Jesus.

Philippians 4:6-7, KJV

Let the peace of Christ rule in your hearts, since as members of one body you were called to peace.

Colossians 3:15, NIV

God is not a God of confusion but of peace.

1 Corinthians 14:33, ESV

Now may the Lord of peace Himself give you peace always in every way.

2 Thessalonians 3:16, NKJV

When a man's ways please the LORD, He makes even his enemies to be at peace with him.

Proverbs 16:7, NKJV

The LORD bless thee, and keep thee: The LORD make his face shine upon thee, and be gracious unto thee: The LORD lift up his countenance upon thee, and give thee peace.

Numbers 6:24-26, KJV

For unto us a Child is born, unto us a Son is given; and the government will be upon His shoulder. And His name will be called Wonderful, Counselor, Mighty God, Everlasting Father, Prince of Peace. Of the increase of His government and peace there will be no end.

Isaiah 9:6-7, NKJV

For He Himself is our peace, who has made both one, and has broken down the middle wall of separation, having abolished in His flesh the enmity, that is, the law of commandments contained in ordinances, so as to create in Himself one new man from the two, thus making peace, and that He might reconcile them both to God in one body through the cross, thereby putting to death the enmity. And He came and preached peace to you who were afar off and to those who were near. For through Him we both have access by one Spirit to the Father.

Ephesians 2:14-18, NKJV

Peacemakers who sow in peace raise a harvest of righteousness.

James 3:18, NIV

PERSEVERANCE

Let us not become weary in doing good, for at the proper time we will reap a harvest if we do not give up.

Galatians 6:9, NIV

We regularly hear of the achievements of sportsmen and women. Much emphasis is placed on the preparation and exercise programs of those who want to achieve the greatest success. Just as the athlete has to prepare himself and has to keep practicing in order to achieve his goals, the Christian should commit Himself to attaining the high standards set by Christ. This calls for courage and steadfast commitment as well as a will of iron and a determination to get to the end. As a Christian, you are assured of the reward you will receive from your Heavenly Father for your commitment and faithfulness – the crown of life.

So hold steadfastly to your faith and do not give up. Complete the race of life in the strength of the Master, and joyfully anticipate the prize of the crown of life that you will have for all eternity.

Hope to

PERSEVERE

Be self-controlled and alert. Your enemy the devil prowls around like a roaring lion looking for someone to devour. Resist him, standing firm in the faith, because you know that your brothers throughout the world are undergoing the same kind of sufferings. And the God of all grace, who called you to his eternal glory in Christ, after you have suffered a little while, will himself restore you and make you strong, firm and steadfast.

1 Peter 5:8-10, NIV

Therefore, since we are surrounded by such a great cloud of witnesses, let us throw off everything that hinders and the sin that so easily entangles, and let us run with perseverance the race marked out for us. Let us fix our eyes on Jesus, the author and perfecter of our faith, who for the joy set before him endured the cross, scorning its shame, and sat down at the right hand of the throne of God. Consider him who endured such opposition from sinful men, so that you will not grow weary and lose heart.

Hebrews 12:1-3, NIV

Wait on the LORD: be of good courage, and he shall strengthen thine heart: wait, I say, on the LORD.

Psalm 27:14, KJV

Behold, we consider those blessed who remained steadfast. You have heard of the steadfastness of Job, and you have seen the purpose of the Lord, how the Lord is compassionate and merciful.

James 5:11, ESV

For we have become partakers of Christ if we hold the beginning of our confidence steadfast to the end.

Hebrews 3:14, NKJV

Stand fast therefore in the liberty wherewith Christ hath made us free, and be not entangled again with the yoke of bondage.

Galatians 5:1, KJV

And take the helmet of salvation, and the sword of the Spirit, which is the word of God; praying always with all prayer and supplication in the Spirit, being watchful to this end with all perseverance and supplication for all the saints.

Ephesians 6:17-18, NKJV

Therefore, my brothers, whom I love and long for, my joy and crown, stand firm thus in the Lord, my beloved.

Philippians 4:1, ESV

I know your deeds, your hard work and your perseverance. I know that you cannot tolerate wicked men, that you have tested those who claim to be apostles but are not, and have found them false. You have persevered and have endured hardships for my name, and have not grown weary.

Revelation 2:2-3, NIV

Count it all joy, my brothers, when you meet trials of various kinds, for you know that the testing of your faith produces steadfastness. And let steadfastness have its full effect, that you may be perfect and complete, lacking in nothing.

James 1:2-4, ESV

Add to your faith virtue, to virtue knowledge, to knowledge self-control, to self-control perseverance, to perseverance godliness, to godliness brotherly kindness, and to brotherly kindness love.

2 Peter 1:5-7, NKJV

PRAISE AND WORSHIP

"Blessing and honor and glory and power be to Him who sits on the throne, and to the Lamb, forever and ever!"

Revelation 5:13, NKJV

Our lives should be a praise offering to God, and we should find opportunities in our daily living to praise Him continuously. But there is something about gathering together with others to praise and worship God that ignites our hearts and souls to a more glorious flame of worship. The Bible tells us that around the throne of God there will be worshipers from every tribe, tongue and nation. Thousands upon thousands will praise Him without ceasing, and oh, how wonderful to have a foretaste of such glory!

He has created all things for His pleasure, and as we worship him, so our pleasure in Him and in His creation is increased. He has given so much to us, and we enjoy all the good things He provides. We offer a sacrifice of praise to Him, a joyful sacrifice, because He has paid in full for our sins, and so we can draw near to Him without fear and without shame.

THE JOY OF

PRAISE AND WORSHIP

I will also praise thee with the psaltery, even thy truth, O my God: unto thee will I sing with the harp, O thou Holy One of Israel. My lips shall greatly rejoice when I sing unto thee; and my soul, which thou hast redeemed.

Psalm 71:22-23, KJV

Is anyone cheerful? Let him sing praise.

James 5:13, ESV

"Yet a time is coming and has now come when the true worshipers will worship the Father in spirit and truth, for they are the kind of worshipers the Father seeks. God is spirit, and his worshipers must worship in spirit and in truth."

John 4:23-24, NIV

Let the word of Christ dwell in you richly, teaching and admonishing one another in all wisdom, singing psalms and hymns and spiritual songs, with thankfulness in your hearts to God.

Colossians 3:16, ESV

Make a joyful noise unto the LORD, all the earth: make a loud noise, and rejoice, and sing praise.

Psalm 98:4, KJV

I will praise You with my whole heart; Before the gods I will sing praises to You. I will worship toward Your holy temple, and praise Your name for Your lovingkindness and Your truth; for You have magnified Your word above all Your name.

Psalm 138:1-2, NKJV

Exalt the LORD our God; worship at his footstool! Holy is he!

Psalm 99:5, ESV

Give to the LORD the glory due His name; bring an offering, and come before Him. Oh, worship the LORD in the beauty of holiness!

1 Chronicles 16:29, NKJV

O LORD, you are my God; I will exalt you and praise your name, for in perfect faithfulness you have done marvelous things, things planned long ago.

Isaiah 25:1, NIV

Praise the LORD, O my soul; all my inmost being, praise his holy name. Praise the LORD, O my soul, and forget not all his benefits.

Psalm 103:1-2, NIV

I will bless the LORD at all times; his praise shall continually be in my mouth. Oh, magnify the LORD with me, and let us exalt his name together!

Psalm 34:1, 3, ESV

By him therefore let us offer the sacrifice of praise to God continually, that is, the fruit of our lips giving thanks to his name.

Hebrews 13:15, KJV

Praise the LORD! Praise God in his sanctuary; praise him in his mighty heavens! Praise him for his mighty deeds; praise him according to his excellent greatness! Praise him with trumpet sound; praise him with lute and harp! Praise him with tambourine and dance; praise him with strings and pipe! Praise him with sounding cymbals; praise him with loud clashing cymbals! Let everything that has breath praise the LORD! Praise the LORD!

Psalm 150:1-6, ESV

PRAYER

"And all things, whatsoever ye shall ask in prayer, believing, ye shall receive."

Matthew 21:22, KJV

Many Christians experience problems with the discipline of prayer. They reason that if God is omniscient, it is not necessary to pray. Yet others feel embarrassed because it seems as if they are continually bothering the Lord with issues which He has known about all along.

If you feel that your case is important enough for action, you ought to lay your request before the Lord. Sincere prayer involves the surrender of yourself, your time and emotions on behalf of someone or something else. God will never tire of your prayers if you pray through Jesus Christ. A father knows what his child needs, without the child having to ask and the father also knows that he can do what the child asks him to. Nevertheless he wants to hear the voice of his child and experience his deep dependency. This is how it is with earthly fathers and also with our heavenly Father.

Promises for those
who pray

"Ask, and it will be given to you; seek, and you will find; knock, and it will be opened to you. For everyone who asks receives, and the one who seeks finds, and to the one who knocks it will be opened."

Matthew 7:7-8, ESV

"But when you pray, go into your room and shut the door and pray to your Father who is in secret. And your Father who sees in secret will reward you."

Matthew 6:6, ESV

The LORD is near to all who call on him, to all who call on him in truth. He fulfills the desires of those who fear him; he hears their cry and saves them.

Psalm 145:18-19, NIV

Do not be anxious about anything, but in everything by prayer and supplication with thanksgiving let your requests be made known to God. And the peace of God, which surpasses all understanding, will guard your hearts and your minds in Christ Jesus.

Philippians 4:6-7, ESV

Therefore I exhort first of all that suppli-
cations, prayers, intercessions, and giving of
thanks be made for all men, for kings and
all who are in authority, that we may lead
a quiet and peaceable life in all godliness
and reverence.

1 Timothy 2:1-2, NKJV

For the people shall dwell in Zion at Jeru-
salem: thou shalt weep no more: he will be
very gracious unto thee at the voice of thy
cry; when he shall hear it, he will answer
thee.

Isaiah 30:19, KJV

"Whatever you ask in my name, this I will
do, that the Father may be glorified in the
Son. If you ask me anything in my name,
I will do it."

John 14:13-14, ESV

Then you will call upon me and come and
pray to me, and I will hear you. You will
seek me and find me. When you seek me
with all your heart, I will be found by you,
declares the LORD.

Jeremiah 29:12-14, ESV

Then you will call, and the LORD will answer; you will cry for help, and he will say: Here am I.

Isaiah 58:9, NIV

"Therefore I tell you, whatever you ask in prayer, believe that you have received it, and it will be yours."

Mark 11:24, ESV

For the eyes of the Lord are over the righteous, and his ears are open unto their prayers: but the face of the Lord is against them that do evil.

1 Peter 3:12, KJV

"Call to Me, and I will answer you, and show you great and mighty things, which you do not know."

Jeremiah 33:3, NKJV

And pray in the Spirit on all occasions with all kinds of prayers and requests. With this in mind, be alert and always keep on praying for all the saints.

Ephesians 6:18, NIV

RELATIONSHIPS

"Love your neighbor as yourself."
Matthew 22:39, NIV

It is rewarding to understand people and to maintain healthy relationships with them. In some cases this is relatively easy, but in others it could be exceptionally difficult. So much depends on the disposition of other people: with some it is easy to start a conversation and their pleasant personalities make it easy to be with them.

There are many people who are abrupt and difficult and who seem to derive pleasure from making things unpleasant for others. You will encounter such people at some stage in your life.

Handling the problem of human relations constructively, requires patience and sympathetic understanding. You need to give others the opportunity to talk and even if what they say hurts, you control the situation by remaining calm. Then you will discover that behind the rough exterior there is a soul that yearns for love and friendship.

Rewarding
RELATIONSHIPS

Finally, be ye all of one mind, having compassion one of another, love as brethren, be pitiful, be courteous: Not rendering evil for evil, or railing for railing: but contrariwise blessing; knowing that ye are thereunto called, that ye should inherit a blessing.

1 Peter 3:8-9, KJV

And we urge you, brethren, to recognize those who labor among you, and are over you in the Lord and admonish you, and to esteem them very highly in love for their work's sake. Be at peace among yourselves.

1 Thessalonians 5:12-13, NKJV

Be kind to one another, tenderhearted, forgiving one another, even as God in Christ forgave you.

Ephesians 4:32, NKJV

Children, obey your parents in the Lord: for this is right. Honour thy father and mother; which is the first commandment with promise.

Ephesians 6:1-2, KJV

Fathers, provoke not your children to wrath: but bring them up in the nurture and admonition of the Lord.

Ephesians 6:4, KJV

"You have heard that it was said, 'You shall love your neighbor and hate your enemy.' But I say to you, Love your enemies and pray for those who persecute you, so that you may be sons of your Father who is in heaven. For he makes his sun rise on the evil and on the good, and sends rain on the just and on the unjust. For if you love those who love you, what reward do you have? Do not even the tax collectors do the same? And if you greet only your brothers, what more are you doing than others? Do not even the Gentiles do the same?"

Matthew 5:43-47, ESV

Servants, be obedient to them that are your masters according to the flesh, with fear and trembling, in singleness of your heart, as unto Christ; and, ye masters, do the same things unto them, forbearing threatening: knowing that your Master also is in heaven; neither is there respect of persons with him.

Ephesians 6:5, 9, KJV

"By this shall all men know that ye are my disciples, if ye have love one to another."

John 13:35, KJV

Two are better than one, because they have a good reward for their labor. For if they fall, one will lift up his companion. But woe to him who is alone when he falls, for he has no one to help him up. Again, if two lie down together, they will keep warm; but how can one be warm alone? Though one may be overpowered by another, two can withstand him. And a threefold cord is not quickly broken.

Ecclesiastes 4:9-12, NKJV

Bear ye one another's burdens, and so fulfil the law of Christ. As we have therefore opportunity, let us do good unto all men, especially unto them who are of the household of faith.

Galatians 6:2, 10, KJV

If we walk in the light, as he is in the light, we have fellowship with one another, and the blood of Jesus, his Son, purifies us from all sin.

1 John 1:7, NIV

RIGHTEOUSNESS

Say to the righteous that it shall be well with them,
for they shall eat the fruit of their doings.

Isaiah 3:10, NKJV

The Gospel brings the news of a righteousness that is acceptable to God. It is His own righteousness. This is available to men because the Son of God was made man and offered Himself without blemish to God. This righteousness is mine by faith because by receiving Jesus Christ as Savior I am made one with Him and all His merits and acceptance become mine also. He who knew no sin was made sin for us, that we who have no righteousness might be made God's righteousness in Him.

This is not by works, that is by our struggling to be better, but by faith, by receiving the Righteous One, Jesus Christ as our own personal Savior. So may we calmly stand in the presence of God because our righteousness is the righteousness of God.

The Word's view

on righteousness

I have fought the good fight, I have finished the race, I have kept the faith. Now there is in store for me the crown of righteousness, which the Lord, the righteous Judge, will award to me on that day – and not only to me, but also to all who have longed for his appearing.

2 Timothy 4:7-8, NIV

"But seek first the kingdom of God and his righteousness, and all these things will be added to you."

Matthew 6:33, ESV

For the LORD God is a sun and shield: the LORD will give grace and glory: no good thing will he withhold from them that walk uprightly.

Psalm 84:11, KJV

Know that the LORD has set apart the godly for himself; the LORD will hear when I call to him.

Psalm 4:3, NIV

"I am the vine; you are the branches. Whoever abides in me and I in him, he it is that bears much fruit, for apart from me you can do nothing. If you abide in me, and my words abide in you, ask whatever you wish, and it will be done for you."

John 15:5, 7, ESV

It is no longer I who live, but Christ who lives in me. And the life I now live in the flesh I live by faith in the Son of God, who loved me and gave himself for me. I do not nullify the grace of God, for if justification were through the law, then Christ died for no purpose.

Galatians 2:20-21, ESV

Treasures of wickedness profit nothing: but righteousness delivereth from death.

Proverbs 10:2, KJV

As righteousness leads to life, so he who pursues evil pursues it to his own death.

Proverbs 11:19, NKJV

Thus says the LORD: "Keep justice, and do righteousness, for soon my salvation will come, and my deliverance be revealed."

Isaiah 56:1, ESV

"Blessed are those who hunger and thirst for righteousness, for they will be filled."

Matthew 5:6, NIV

And the work of righteousness shall be peace; and the effect of righteousness quietness and assurance for ever.

Isaiah 32:17, KJV

It is because of him that you are in Christ Jesus, who has become for us wisdom from God – that is, our righteousness, holiness and redemption.

1 Corinthians 1:30, NIV

And a harvest of righteousness is sown in peace by those who make peace.

James 3:18, ESV

Finally, there is laid up for me the crown of righteousness, which the Lord, the righteous Judge, will give to me on that Day, and not to me only but also to all who have loved His appearing.

2 Timothy 4:8, NKJV

$\mathcal{S}$IN

Blessed is the one whose transgression is forgiven, whose sin is covered.

Psalm 32:1, ESV

Because Christ understands your weaknesses, it doesn't mean that He condones your sins. He, who was tempted like us in all respects, has called you to a life of victory through the power of His Holy Spirit. Those things which people call "weaknesses" for convenience, sake, but which are really just sins, rob our spiritual life of its growth and vigor.

As far as Christ is concerned there are no insignificant sins, because all sin separates us from God. Christ never tries to gloss over sin. He understands human weakness and frailty, offers forgiveness, and purifies us, saves us, and gives us the spiritual strength to live victoriously.

Christ looks beyond man's sin and sees what he can become through the power of God's Holy Spirit. Because He knows what people are like, He knows their potential and desires to lead them to the perfection that God has ordained for them.

The Word's view

on sin

For all have sinned, and come short of the glory of God; being justified freely by his grace through the redemption that is in Christ Jesus: whom God hath set forth to be a propitiation through faith in his blood, to declare his righteousness for the remission of sins that are past, through the forbearance of God.

Romans 3:23-25, KJV

In him you were also circumcised, in the putting off of the sinful nature, not with a circumcision done by the hands of men but with the circumcision done by Christ, having been buried with him in baptism and raised with him through your faith in the power of God, who raised him from the dead. When you were dead in your sins and in the uncircumcision of your sinful nature, God made you alive with Christ. He forgave us all our sins, having canceled the written code, with its regulations, that was against us and that stood opposed to us; he took it away, nailing it to the cross.

Colossians 2:11-14, NIV

Surely there is not a righteous man on earth who does good and never sins.

Ecclesiastes 7:20, ESV

"For God so loved the world that He gave His only begotten Son, that whoever believes in Him should not perish but have everlasting life. For God did not send His Son into the world to condemn the world, but that the world through Him might be saved."

John 3:16-17, NKJV

He himself bore our sins in his body on the tree, so that we might die to sins and live for righteousness; by his wounds you have been healed.

1 Peter 2:24, NIV

If we say we have no sin, we deceive ourselves, and the truth is not in us. If we confess our sins, he is faithful and just to forgive us our sins and to cleanse us from all unrighteousness.

1 John 1:8-9, ESV

"This is my blood of the covenant, which is poured out for many for the forgiveness of sins."

Matthew 26:28, NIV

Therefore let it be known to you, brethren, that through this Man is preached to you the forgiveness of sins; and by Him everyone who believes is justified from all things from which you could not be justified by the law.

Acts 13:38-39, NKJV

I will sprinkle clean water on you, and you will be clean; I will cleanse you from all your impurities and from all your idols. I will give you a new heart and put a new spirit in you; I will remove from you your heart of stone and give you a heart of flesh. And I will put my Spirit in you and move you to follow my decrees and be careful to keep my laws.

Ezekiel 36:25-27, NIV

Therefore if any man be in Christ, he is a new creature: old things are passed away; behold, all things are become new.

2 Corinthians 5:17, KJV

So you also must consider yourselves dead to sin and alive to God in Christ Jesus. Let not sin therefore reign in your mortal bodies, to make you obey their passions. For sin will have no dominion over you, since you are not under law but under grace.

Romans 6:11-12, 14, ESV

$\mathcal{S}$UCCESS

Every man also to whom God hath given riches and wealth, and hath given him power to eat thereof, and to take his portion, and to rejoice in his labour; this is the gift of God.

Ecclesiastes 5:19, KJV

Success means different things to different people. Yet there are basic characteristics that can be identified. Success is utilizing every day to the full, not putting off for tomorrow what can be done today.

Success is knowing your limitations and seeing them as challenges, not as stumbling blocks. God has given different gifts to different people, and He expects me to do my best. My limitations should inspire me to give more of myself, to do more than just the minimum required.

Success requires hard work. There are no shortcuts to success. Success is to place God first in your life. If God has the place of honor in your life and you approach life from His perspective, success is sure to follow.

The Word's view

on success

And the LORD will grant you plenty of goods, in the fruit of your body, in the increase of your livestock, and in the produce of your ground, in the land of which the LORD swore to your fathers to give you. The LORD will open to you His good treasure, the heavens, to give the rain to your land in its season, and to bless all the work of your hand. You shall lend to many nations, but you shall not borrow. And the LORD will make you the head and not the tail; you shall be above only, and not be beneath, if you heed the commandments of the LORD your God, which I command you today, and are careful to observe them.

Deuteronomy 28:11-13, NKJV

Blessed is the man who does not walk in the counsel of the wicked or stand in the way of sinners or sit in the seat of mockers. He is like a tree planted by streams of water, which yields its fruit in season and whose leaf does not wither. Whatever he does prospers.

Psalm 1:1, 3, NIV

No longer will they build houses and others live in them, or plant and others eat. For as the days of a tree, so will be the days of my people; my chosen ones will long enjoy the works of their hands. They will not toil in vain or bear children doomed to misfortune; for they will be a people blessed by the LORD, they and their descendants with them.

Isaiah 65:22-23, NIV

Blessed is everyone who fears the LORD, who walks in his ways! You shall eat the fruit of the labor of your hands; you shall be blessed, and it shall be well with you.

Psalm 128:1-2, ESV

Praise ye the LORD. Blessed is the man that feareth the LORD, that delighteth greatly in his commandments. His seed shall be mighty upon earth: the generation of the upright shall be blessed. Wealth and riches shall be in his house: and his righteousness endureth for ever.

Psalm 112:1-3, KJV

The reward for humility and fear of the LORD is riches and honor and life.

Proverbs 22:4, ESV

"For I know the plans I have for you," declares the LORD, "plans to prosper you and not to harm you, plans to give you hope and a future."

Jeremiah 29:11, NIV

And also that every man should eat and drink, and enjoy the good of all his labour, it is the gift of God.

Ecclesiastes 3:13, KJV

The LORD was with Joseph and gave him success in whatever he did.

Genesis 39:23, NIV

This Book of the Law shall not depart from your mouth, but you shall meditate in it day and night, that you may observe to do according to all that is written in it. For then you will make your way prosperous, and then you will have good success.

Joshua 1:8, NKJV

WEAKNESS

"My grace is sufficient for you, for my power is made perfect in weakness."

2 Corinthians 12:9, NIV

Scripture contains Christ's invitation to those who are tired and heavy-laden, to bring their problems to Him so that they may find rest for their souls. His Word also extends an invitation to you to bring your anxious cares to Him, because He cares for you. Right through the Bible you are invited to turn to God in Christ so that in His omnipotence He can enable you to handle your problems with confidence.

Regardless of what your circumstances in life may be, don't run away from them in panic and despair, but contend with them with Christ at your side. Receive your strength and confidence from Him. Regardless of how alarming the problem may seem, know for sure that God's omnipotence will be revealed in your weakness. Under all circumstances His grace will be sufficient for you so that you can deal with your problems with His strength.

GOD'S STRENGTH

FOR THE WEAK

Fear thou not; for I am with thee: be not dismayed; for I am thy God: I will strengthen thee; yea, I will help thee; yea, I will uphold thee with the right hand of my righteousness.

Isaiah 41:10, KJV

I pray that out of his glorious riches he may strengthen you with power through his Spirit in your inner being, so that Christ may dwell in your hearts through faith.

Ephesians 3:16-17, NIV

I will seek the lost, and I will bring back the strayed, and I will bind up the injured, and I will strengthen the weak, and the fat and the strong I will destroy. I will feed them in justice.

Ezekiel 34:16, ESV

The LORD is my strength and song, and he is become my salvation: he is my God, and I will prepare him an habitation; my father's God, and I will exalt him.

Exodus 15:2, KJV

My hand will sustain him; surely my arm will strengthen him.

Psalm 89:21, NIV

But the God of all grace, who hath called us unto his eternal glory by Christ Jesus, after that ye have suffered a while, make you perfect, stablish, strengthen, settle you.

1 Peter 5:10, KJV

Have you not known? Have you not heard? The everlasting God, the LORD, the Creator of the ends of the earth, neither faints nor is weary. His understanding is unsearchable. He gives power to the weak, and to those who have no might He increases strength. Even the youths shall faint and be weary, and the young men shall utterly fall, but those who wait on the LORD shall renew their strength; they shall mount up with wings like eagles, they shall run and not be weary, they shall walk and not faint.

Isaiah 40:28-31, NKJV

It is God that girdeth me with strength, and maketh my way perfect. He maketh my feet like hinds' feet, and setteth me upon my high places.

Psalm 18:32-33, KJV

My flesh and my heart may fail, but God is the strength of my heart and my portion forever.

Psalm 73:26, NIV

The LORD will give strength unto his people; the LORD will bless his people with peace.

Psalm 29:11, KJV

Have mercy on me, O LORD, for I am weak; O LORD, heal me, for my bones are troubled.

Psalm 6:2, NKJV

Behold, thou hast instructed many, and thou hast strengthened the weak hands.

Job 4:3, KJV

Be strong and of good courage, do not fear nor be afraid of them; for the LORD your God, He is the One who goes with you. He will not leave you nor forsake you.

Deuteronomy 31:6, NKJV

Finally, my brethren, be strong in the Lord, and in the power of his might.

Ephesians 6:10, KJV

Wisdom

With Him are wisdom and strength, He has counsel and understanding.

Job 12:13, NKJV

Wisdom is the practical application of knowledge, understanding is the appreciation of the true character of things. A wise and understanding man appreciates the true nature of a situation and applies his knowledge to meet it. But where, or by whom, are these qualities dispensed?

The wealth of knowledge and the ability to apply the knowledge is in Christ, who not only possesses these desirable gifts but makes them available to all who are united to Him by faith. If therefore we are in Christ we are in closest touch with wisdom and at the very center of understanding.

No servant of God can pride himself that he is able to assess the nature of things and apply his knowledge to needs and problems. His trust must be in the only wise God whose wisdom is available to him, because, by grace, he is found in Christ Jesus.

Wisdom from the Word

Yea, if thou criest after knowledge, and liftest up thy voice for understanding; if thou seekest her as silver, and searchest for her as for hid treasures; then shalt thou understand the fear of the LORD, and find the knowledge of God. For the LORD giveth wisdom: out of his mouth cometh knowledge and understanding. He layeth up sound wisdom for the righteous: he is a buckler to them that walk uprightly.

Proverbs 2:3-7, KJV

If any of you lacks wisdom, let him ask of God, who gives to all liberally and without reproach, and it will be given to him.

James 1:5, NKJV

Listen to advice and accept instruction, that you may gain wisdom in the future.

Proverbs 19:20, ESV

I will instruct thee and teach thee in the way which thou shalt go: I will guide thee with mine eye.

Psalm 32:8, KJV

I will praise the LORD, who counsels me; even at night my heart instructs me.

Psalm 16:7, NIV

"But where can wisdom be found? Where does understanding dwell? Man does not comprehend its worth; it cannot be found in the land of the living. It cannot be bought with the finest gold, nor can its price be weighed in silver. Where then does wisdom come from? Where does understanding dwell? It is hidden from the eyes of every living thing, concealed even from the birds of the air. God understands the way to it and he alone knows where it dwells, for he views the ends of the earth and sees everything under the heavens."

Job 28:12-13, 15, 20-21, 23-24, NIV

For God giveth to a man that is good in his sight, wisdom, and knowledge, and joy.

Ecclesiastes 2:26, KJV

But the wisdom that is from above is first pure, then peaceable, gentle, willing to yield, full of mercy and good fruits, without partiality and without hypocrisy.

James 3:17, NKJV

The fear of the LORD is the beginning of wisdom; all those who practice it have a good understanding. His praise endures forever!

Psalm 111:10, ESV

Oh, the depth of the riches of the wisdom and knowledge of God! How unsearchable his judgments, and his paths beyond tracing out!

Romans 11:33, NIV

Who has put wisdom in the mind? Or who has given understanding to the heart? Who can number the clouds by wisdom?

Job 38:36-37, NKJV

Who is wise and understanding among you? Let him show it by his good life, by deeds done in the humility that comes from wisdom.

James 3:13, NIV

Wisdom is the principal thing; therefore get wisdom. And in all your getting, get understanding.

Proverbs 4:7, NKJV

WORK

Whatsoever thy hand findeth to do, do it with thy might.

Ecclesiastes 9:10, KJV

Some people find that their daily work becomes dull and monotonous. They lose their joy and inspiration, and become negative and cynical. There are many reasons that can lead to this attitude: insufficient rest and relaxation; carrying a burden of responsibility beyond your ability. Tension and stress then play havoc with your nerves and you develop a grudge against your job.

This may be because you are trying to live and work without the power of Jesus Christ. Remember that Jesus said "without me you can do nothing" (Jn. 15:5).

The best way to ensure maximum productivity without stress is to remember that Jesus is your partner in work as well as at church. Surrender every aspect of your life to Him. Start each day in His presence and then go into the world knowing that His presence will go with you.

THE WORD'S VIEW

ON WORK

A slack hand causes poverty, but the hand of the diligent makes rich.

Proverbs 10:4, ESV

"He that is faithful in that which is least is faithful also in much: and he that is unjust in the least is unjust also in much."

Luke 16:10, KJV

The sleep of a laborer is sweet.

Ecclesiastes 5:12, NIV

Whatever you do, work heartily, as for the Lord and not for men, knowing that from the Lord you will receive the inheritance as your reward. You are serving the Lord Christ.

Colossians 3:23-24, ESV

Let the favor of the LORD our God be upon us, and establish the work of our hands upon us; yes, establish the work of our hands!

Psalm 90:17, ESV

For other foundation can no man lay than that is laid, which is Jesus Christ. Now if any man build upon this foundation gold, silver, precious stones, wood, hay, stubble; every man's work shall be made manifest: for the day shall declare it, because it shall be revealed by fire; and the fire shall try every man's work of what sort it is. If any man's work abide which he hath built thereupon, he shall receive a reward.

1 Corinthians 3:11-14, KJV

Six days thou shalt work, but on the seventh day thou shalt rest: in earing time and in harvest thou shalt rest.

Exodus 34:21, KJV

Whatever you do, whether in word or deed, do it all in the name of the Lord Jesus, giving thanks to God the Father through him.

Colossians 3:17, NIV

With good will doing service, as to the Lord, and not to men: knowing that whatsoever good thing any man doeth, the same shall he receive of the Lord, whether he be bond or free.

Ephesians 6:7-8, KJV

Whoever is slack in his work is a brother to him who destroys.

Proverbs 18:9, ESV

Who can find a virtuous woman? for her price is far above rubies. She seeketh wool, and flax, and worketh willingly with her hands. She is like the merchants' ships; she bringeth her food from afar. Give her of the fruit of her hands; and let her own works praise her in the gates.

Proverbs 31:10, 13-14, 31, KJV

Therefore, my beloved brethren, be steadfast, immovable, always abounding in the work of the Lord, knowing that your labor is not in vain in the Lord.

1 Corinthians 15:58, NKJV

For even when we were with you, we would give you this command: If anyone is not willing to work, let him not eat. For we hear that some among you walk in idleness, not busy at work, but busybodies. Now such persons we command and encourage in the Lord Jesus Christ to do their work quietly and to earn their own living.

2 Thessalonians 3:10-12, ESV

WORRY

"Let not your hearts be troubled. Believe in God; believe also in me."

John 14:1, ESV

There are few things that have such a negative effect on your spiritual, physical and emotional well-being as problems and worries. They influence your mind to such an extent that your mental abilities may be impaired. In many cases this results in people becoming spiritual and physical wrecks.

When Jesus called those who are weary and overburdened to Him He did not promise that all their problems would disappear instantaneously. Instead, he offered to share your burden and also to teach you how to cope with it.

You cannot predict when you will experience setbacks in life, nor can you foresee how serious these incidents will be. What is of crucial importance is that you prepare yourself to handle these problems when they crop up. To maintain peace of mind, it is essential to develop a healthy personal relationship with the living Christ.

THE WORD'S VIEW

ON WORRY

When the cares of my heart are many, your consolations cheer my soul.

Psalm 94:19, ESV

Do not be anxious about anything, but in everything, by prayer and petition, with thanksgiving, present your requests to God. And the peace of God, which transcends all understanding, will guard your hearts and your minds in Christ Jesus.

Philippians 4:6-7, NIV

"Do not worry about your life, what you will eat or what you will drink; nor about your body, what you will put on. Is not life more than food and the body more than clothing? Look at the birds of the air, for they neither sow nor reap nor gather into barns; yet your heavenly Father feeds them. Are you not of more value than they? Which of you by worrying can add one cubit to his stature?"

Matthew 6:25-27, NKJV

Humble yourselves, therefore, under the mighty hand of God so that at the proper time he may exalt you, casting all your anxieties on him, because he cares for you.

1 Peter 5:6-7, ESV

An anxious heart weighs a man down, but a kind word cheers him up.

Proverbs 12:25, NIV

"So why do you worry about clothing? Consider the lilies of the field, how they grow: they neither toil nor spin; and yet I say to you that even Solomon in all his glory was not arrayed like one of these. Now if God so clothes the grass of the field, which today is, and tomorrow is thrown into the oven, will He not much more clothe you, O you of little faith? Therefore do not worry, saying, 'What shall we eat?' or 'What shall we drink?' or 'What shall we wear?' For after all these things the Gentiles seek. For your heavenly Father knows that you need all these things. Therefore do not worry about tomorrow, for tomorrow will worry about its own things."

Matthew 6:28-32, 34, NKJV

"Come to me, all you who are weary and burdened, and I will give you rest. Take my yoke upon you and learn from me, for I am gentle and humble in heart, and you will find rest for your souls. For my yoke is easy and my burden is light."

Mattthew 11:28-30, NIV

He who dwells in the shelter of the Most High will abide in the shadow of the Almighty. I will say to the LORD, "My refuge and my fortress, my God, in whom I trust."

Psalm 91:1-2, ESV

Carry each other's burdens, and in this way you will fulfill the law of Christ.

Galatians 6:2, NIV

Why art thou cast down, O my soul? and why art thou disquieted within me? Hope in God: for I shall yet praise him, who is the health of my countenance, and my God.

Psalm 43:5, KJV

Sources

The devotions included in this book have been drawn from the following sources:

1. Mitchell, Fred. 1968. *At Break of Day, Marshall.* Morgan and Scott.
2. Murray, Andrew. 2002. *Humility.* Vereeniging: Christian Art Publishers.
3. Ozrovech, Solly. 2002. *Fountains of Blessing.* Vereeniging: Christian Art Publishers.
4. Ozrovech, Solly. 2000. *The Glory of God's Grace.* Vereeniging: Christian Art Publishers.
5. Ozrovech, Solly. 2000. *Intimate Moments with God.* Vereeniging: Christian Art Publishers.
6. Ozrovech, Solly. 2000. *New Beginnings.* Vereeniging: Christian Art Publishers.
7. Ozrovech, Solly. 2002. *The Voice Behind You.* Vereeniging: Christian Art Publishers.
8. Tileston, Mary (compiler). 1951. *Daily Strength for Daily Needs.* London: Methuen.

OTHER BOOKS

IN THIS RANGE

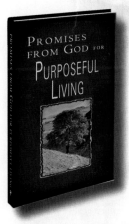 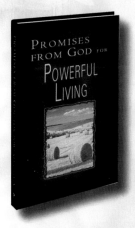

ISBN: 978-1-86920-536-2   ISBN: 978-1-86920-537-9

ISBN: 978-1-86920-070-1